LUDWIG CURTIUS

ROME

AN ILLUSTRATED SELECTIVE GUIDE TO ALL IMPORTANT ART TREASURES IN ROME AND ITS ENVIRONS

PANTHEON

Photographs by ERNEST NASH

Printed by Belgrave Press, New York, U. S. A.

PREFACE

THE TRAVELER with only a few fleeting days for Rome cannot expect to acquaint himself with the city thoroughly. He cannot visit all the churches, linger before all the monuments that span the more than two millennia of the city's history, nor study the productions of all the architects, sculptors, and painters whose work gave the city its character. He must limit himself to the contemplation of only the most important monuments. It is better to enjoy a little, and in tranquillity, than to dash past a great deal and then promptly forget a mass of uncoordinated impressions.

This little book is designed as an aid to such a selective tour. It contains no practical instructions on hotels, banks, transportation, and the like. Such matters are adequately cared for by numerous excellent travel agencies. It is the object of this book to introduce the traveler to Rome's historical and spiritual environment, and in the briefest possible compass.

In order to avoid repetition of dates in the text, lists of Popes, Emperors and artists mentioned in the book, with their dates, are appended.

VISITING HOURS

Baths of Caracalla (Terme di Caracalla), Passeggiata Archeologica: 10 A.M. to 4 P.M.

Catacombs of S. Callisto, Via Appia No. 110: 8 A.M. to 12 P.M. and 2 P.M. to sundown.

Farnesina, Via della Lungara: 10 A.M. to 4 P.M.

FORA

   Roman Forum, Via dei Fori Imperiali: 9 A.M. to sundown.
   Imperial Fora: 10 A.M. to 4 P.M.

MUSEUMS

   Museo and *Galleria Borghese*, Villa Borghese: 9 A.M. to 2 P.M.; holidays, 10 A.M. to 1 P.M. Closed Mondays.

   Museo Capitolino and *Museo dei Conservatori*, Piazza di Campidoglio: 9 A.M. to 2 P.M.; holidays, 10 A.M. to 1 P.M.

   Museo del Laterano, Piazza S. Giovanni in Laterano: Weekdays, with the exception of Monday, from 9 A.M. to 2 P.M. Sundays from 2 P.M. (Oct. 1 to March 31) and 3 P.M. (April 1 to Sept. 30) until ½ hour before sundown.

   Museo Nazionale Romano or *delle Terme*, Viale delle Terme: 9 A.M. to 2 P.M.; holidays, 10 A.M. to 1 P.M.

   Museo Nazionale di Villa Giulia, Viale delle Belle Arti: 9 A.M. to 2 P.M.; holidays, 10 A.M. to 1 P.M.

   Vatican City Museums and Galleries, Viale Vaticano: Weekdays, 9 A.M. to 2 P.M. Closed on Sundays and holidays.

Ostia Excavations: 9 A.M. to sundown.

VILLE

   ROME: *Villa Medici*, Piazza Trinità dei Monti: Garden open to visitors Wednesdays and Saturdays, 2 P.M. to 4 P.M. *Villa Albani*, now *Torlonia*, 92 Via Salaria: Special permit from Principe Torlonia, Via Tomacelli 139.

   FRASCATI: *Ville Aldobrandini, Lancellotti, Falconieri, Mondragone* and *Torlonia*: Permits for visiting have to be secured at the Agency of the Banco dello Spirito, Piazza Monte Grappa, Rome.

   TIVOLI: *Villa d'Este*: 9 A.M. to 6 P.M. *Villa Gregoriana*: 8.30 A.M. to 5 P.M.

   Villa Adriana: 9 A.M. to sundown.

CONTENTS

EXCURSIONS IN THE VICINITY OF ROME

THE HISTORY OF ROME

Romans still celebrate April 21, 753 B.C. as their city's birthday, but the date is legendary rather than historical. Rome, the ancient *City of the Seven Hills*, arose out of small peasant villages. These lay on the *Palatine*, the *Quirinal*, and the *Esquiline* hills. The *Capitoline* hill, between the Palatine and the Quirinal, afforded too little space for a settlement, but its declivities were defensible, and in times of war it became a place of refuge. To these four hills were joined the *Aventine*, where the venerable Medieval Church of Santa Sabina still survives; the *Caelian*, with the Church of San Gregorio Magno, going back to the great Pope Gregory I, and the *Viminal*, where the modern traveler arrives by rail.

The Palatine hill dominates the navigable Tiber. An ancient highway from the south passed northward through Rome. Volcanic soil rendered the surrounding countryside fertile. Rome's dominant position thus was the result of these favorable geographical conditions.

The name of Rome is Etruscan. The Etruscans, an ancient people about whom little is known to this day, originally possessed all central Italy. The name of their capital, Tarquinii, modern Tarquinia, recurs in the names of two Roman kings. But the Romans were not Etruscans. They were an immigrant people who crossed the Alps from northern Europe. Their language belongs to the Indo-European family, as do Greek, Celtic, German, and English.

Numerous minor tribes and cities of the region called Latium, in the plain extending from the Alban Hills to the mouth of the Tiber and beyond, were united by Rome. In the earliest period, Rome was governed for about 200 years by kings, a senate (council of elders), and an assembly of burghers. To this period belongs the Law of the Twelve Tables, inscribed upon bronze plaques and affixed to the speaker's platform (rostra) in the Roman Forum for all to read. It is our first information concerning the Roman law, which was developed and extended in the centuries following. Upon it is based the codification of law and its scientific elaboration in all civilized countries of the modern world.

Rome's neighbors to the south were the Greek colonial cities of southern Italy. The Etruscans, too, were steeped in Greek culture. Hence from north and south alike the sober practicality of the Roman character was early exposed to Greek religion and Greek cultural patterns. In the Roman Forum stood statues of the philosopher Pythagoras, "the wisest of the Greeks," and of Alcibiades, "the bravest of the Greeks." The most ancient Temple of Jupiter Capitolinus was erected on the Capitoline hill in 509 B.C. in Greek-Etruscan form. That same year Rome concluded its first commercial treaty with its powerful rival, the Phoenician commercial Republic Carthage, on the North-African coast, and thus secured commercial domination of Latium. The year 510 B.C. marks the fall of Tarquinius Superbus, Rome's last king. From then on, for about 500 years, Rome was governed by the senate, as a Republic.

Ancient Rome consumed Italy piece by piece. The rich Etruscan cities to the north and the stalwart hill peoples to the south were subdued, and incorporated under the dominion of Rome. As a symbol of the victory over the Latin League, the bronze beaks of ships captured at Anzio were affixed to the rostra in the Forum in 338 B.C. The war against the flourishing Greek colonial city of Tarentum (modern Taranto) brought Rome her richest booty in the south of the peninsula. The construction of the great roads, which still serve traffic today and which were unparalleled in antiquity, demonstrates Rome's reach to the south and to the north. In 312 B.C. Appius Claudius, general, and fervently democratic statesman, constructed the first Roman road from Rome to Capua; this was the Via Appia, which was later extended to Brindisi. In 220 B.C. Caius Flaminius, whose politics resembled Appius', built the Via Flaminia which leads from Rome beyond the Apennines to Rimini in upper Italy. (Rimini was an outpost against the gallant and fiery Celts who, as a prelude to the later migrations of the Germans, flooded Europe, even occupying Rome in 390 B.C., and eventually settled down in upper Italy.)

The Celts were the strongest allies of Hannibal, the Carthaginian general who, in the perennial quarrel of Rome with the Phoenician Republic of Carthage, invaded Italy by way of Spain and the Alps, and destroyed Roman armies, first at the Trasimene Lake north of Rome in 217 B.C., and then at Cannae in Apulia near Barletta in 216 B.C. Rome was never greater than in this crisis which threatened annihilation. After persevering through three wars against Carthage, Rome conquered Carthage in 146 B.C., and thus acquired the province of Africa. In 144 B.C. followed the conquest of Greece, Spain, and southern France, and of Dalmatia and upper Italy, which was still inhabited by Gauls. In a second prelude to the migrations of peoples, the Cimbri and Teutones, Germanic tribes, irrupted into southern France, Spain, and finally upper Italy, until the Roman senator and general, Marius, succeeded in destroying them at Vercellae in 101.

The incessant wars cost Rome her most precious asset, the peasants. The peasant could not serve for decades as soldier and cultivate his farm at the same time. The immense wealth which streamed into Rome through trade, war booty, and exploitation of the provinces, profited not the people, but a small group of aristocratic families who, in the Republic, directed policy as senators and elected officials at home, and as generals abroad. There arose a deep social cleavage between a proletariat, hungry for land, and a noble plutocracy, split by its internal rivalries. Frightful civil wars in the first century B.C. were the consequence. These gave rise to the military dictatorship of the highly gifted Julius Caesar, who, by his conquest of Gaul, had acquired the wealth and the army which afforded him access to power. In the war with his rival for power, Pompey and his adherents, Caesar conquered Egypt and the western portion of North Africa. But the execution of his grandiose plans for the transformation of the Roman Empire was prevented by his assassination at the hands of the conspiratorial defenders of the ancient Republic in 44 B.C. What he had begun was completed by his nephew and adoptive son, Augustus. In 42 B.C. Augustus defeated the anti-dictatorial party at Philippi, and in commemoration of his victory erected the Temple and the Forum of Augustus, dedicated to Mars the Avenger (p. 28). But it was only after his victory over another rival for dictatorial powers, the General Marc Antony, at Actium in 31 B.C., and the death of Queen Cleopatra of Egypt, that his sole dominion was assured. Augustus was one of the greatest statesmen of all time. Preserving the external democratic and republican forms, he united all the military and civil power in his own person. He possessed a remarkable sense of the achievable. After the devastation of more than a half-century of civil war he endeavored to unite all forces for the reconstruction of the state. He was Rome's first great builder. He completed the edifices begun by Caesar and could well say that he had transformed Rome from a city of mud brick into a city of marble.

With Augustus begins a period of peace for the countries of the Mediterranean and gradually also for the entire Roman Empire which lasted for more than two centuries, and the like of which the world has never again seen. Fully to understand Rome's effort and contribution we must realize that Italy, which today has a population of forty-five millions, had scarcely more than ten million inhabitants under Augustus. The city of Rome numbered scarcely a million. The penetration of the northern countries—France, England, Germany—by the Roman culture of what had now become the Roman Empire laid the foundation for the civilization of Europe.

One who inspects the remains of Rome must rid himself of the popular illusion that the Romans early grew decadent and that the Roman Emperors were devoted only to pleasure. Of the forty Roman Emperors from Augustus (27 B.C.-14 A.D.) to Constantine the Great (323-337 A.D.) only five died a natural death in the Imperial palace on the Palatine. Besides madmen like Caligula, Nero, and Domitian, who were destroyed by their own folly, the series of Roman Emperors displays characters of the greatest military and political energy, like Vespasian and Trajan, Marcus Aurelius and Septimius Severus, Aurelian and Diocletian.

The causes for the gradual decline of the Roman Empire cannot be blamed on individual Emperors. They were more deep-seated. The first calamity was that neither Augustus nor his successors were able to establish a regular succession within their families. The result was chronic insurrection against the Imperial office, which was always felt to be illegal. Palace revolutions and dubious successions, with their aftermath of civil strife, cost the best blood of the ancient aristocracy.

A second cause was the enormous expansion of the Empire, the defense of which drained its military and financial resources. After Augustus the Roman Empire suffered from two open wounds which never wholly cicatrized, despite every effort to heal them. One was the onset of eastern peoples, first the Parthians, then the Persians, and finally the Arabs and Turks. The other was the onset of the German tribes. Their destruction of a Roman army in the Teutoburg Forest in 9 A.D. had already forced Augustus to give up his plan to extend the Empire beyond the Rhine. In the middle of the 3rd century A.D. German tribes streamed over Gaul and threatened Spain and Italy. By the end of the 3rd century difficulties of defense forced Emperor Diocletian to divide the Imperial administration. One Emperor resided at Treves on the Moselle River, another at Milan, and Diocletian himself in Nicomedia in Asia Minor. Constantine the Great removed his residence to Constantinople. At Rome, Diocletian still constructed

5

his Baths and Constantine completed the Basilica in the Forum, and his triumphal arch. In 271 Emperor Aurelian endeavored to defend Rome against the threatening incursions of the Germans, erecting a wall, parts of which are still standing. But Rome's role as hub of the Empire was finished.

Rome was by then the most magnificent city in the world. It contained 856 baths, great and small, 290 granaries for public alimentation, eight large libraries, 1352 monumental fountains which were fed by eleven aqueducts. In 410 A.D. the Gothic king, Alaric, leading his Visigoths to a second invasion of Italy, conquered the city. A new section of its history dates from this time. The Roman-Imperial city gradually became the Medieval Christian Rome of the Popes.

Christianity, arisen in Palestine through the example, the teachings, and the death of Jesus, could not have spread over the world without the framework of the Greek and Latin languages and the peace of the Roman Empire. The arrival at Rome of the Apostles Peter and Paul and their martyrdom mark the rise of Rome to the role of focus of the new Church. Christianity established its superiority over the numerous other religions of the Roman Empire by its tenets of a purer and loftier personal morality, by its consciousness of uninterrupted contact with God, and by the practice of neighborly love to all men. The new social and philanthropic character of Christianity gave rise to a new cohesion among its faithful, and to an activity of social welfare on the part of the clergy such as had been unknown to pagan Rome. The weaker Rome became—its borders attacked, its wealth lost, its state forms mummified—the more important did the new social organization of the Christian Church become. It was this importance which determined the Emperor Constantine, after his victory over the rival Emperor Maxentius at the Milvian Bridge in Rome in 312 A.D., to embrace Christianity and to grant complete religious freedom in the Edict of Milan. The oldest Christian basilica in Rome, that of S. Giovanni in Laterano, the First Church of Saint

Peter after 324-25, the Church of the Apostles on the site of the catacombs on the Via Appia (the modern S. Sebastiano), are all foundations of Constantine. These and the numerous constructions of his successors, and of the papacy which gradually grew to world power, and the basilicas of which those of S. Paolo fuori le Mura (p. 90) built in 386, and Santa Maria Maggiore, built in the first half of the 5th century (p. 71), are the most important, gradually transformed ancient pagan Rome into the Christian Rome of the Middle Ages.

Roman rule of Italy came to an end with the conquest of the peninsula by the new German invaders under Odoacer and the deposition of the Emperor Romulus Augustulus in 476. Now Rome was impoverished and outside the main stream of history. It was never ravaged by the peoples of the migrations, but its ancient temples and monuments were neglected and gradually fell to ruin, and its hills were deserted. After the Gothic wars in the 6th century its population had shrunk to some 35,000 souls.

In the centuries following, the prestige and power of the papacy rose increasingly. The Roman Church, through various gifts, possessed property and territorial possessions which in the course of time became concentrated in and around Rome. The Popes, ever more active in the government and defense of the city and province of Rome, finally achieved a kind of sovereignty in the domain sacred to Saint Peter. It was felt that its administration should be entrusted to Saint Peter's successor, the Pope. In the eighth century, the Pope put himself, for purposes of defense against the encroaching Lombards, under the protection of the Frankish princes, then the most powerful rulers in Europe. To his Roman possessions were added, in Italy, the exarchate of Ravenna and some other districts in central Italy. This was the foundation of the Papal States, which survived until the unification of Italy into a modern state in the 19th century.

Having become a temporal power, the papacy was soon involved in conflicts with other temporal powers, the German and French princes in particular. These conflicts culminated in a change of the traditional papal seat from Rome to Avignon in France, decided upon by the French Pope Clement V in 1309, in order to make ecclesiastical government independent of the party strife and warfare raging in Italy. Actually, this step weakened the influence of the Church considerably by removing Church administration from its natural center. With Clement V starts the so-called Babylonian Exile of the Popes, which lasted well into the 14th century. In 1377 Pope Gregory XI finally returned definitely to Rome.

The return of the Popes and the influence of the great spiritual, artistic, and political ferment of the Renaissance mark a new efflorescence for Rome. A new awareness of human values was promoted by the rediscovery and study of treasures of Roman and Greek literature. Petrarch and Boccaccio produced a new lyric poetry and a new narrative technique; Macchiavelli a new theory of the state. Art-loving Popes from Nicholas V onwards drew the artistic talent of Italy to Rome. Under their influence the Rome of the Middle Ages was transformed into the Rome of the Renaissance: new streets and quarters, churches and palaces, altar decorations and frescoes came into being. Julius II and Leo X, who employed the greatest architects, sculptors, and painters in the construction and decoration of the new Saint Peter's and the new Vatican Palace (pp. 42, 49) mark the high point of this development.

The political aspirations of the papacy, which had alternately supported the kingdom of France and the Spanish-Hapsburg monarchy, the two great powers of Europe, were crushed by Charles V of Spain, whose troops sacked Rome in 1527. Catholic unity was broken by the Reformation of Martin Luther and of Zwingli and Calvin, which rapidly spread over Germany, France, Switzerland, England, and the Scandinavian countries. But the Church rallied its forces through the Jesuit order, confirmed by Paul III at the Council of Trent (1545-1563), and through the organization of the Counter Reformation. The Popes devoted themselves to their spiritual tasks and to the artistic beautification of Rome. Sixtus V built a new quarter on the deserted hills from the Pincio to Santa Maria Maggiore on the Esquiline. The Baroque period in architecture, sculpture, and painting, which begins at the end of the 16th century, attained its full flower in the 17th century with Maderna, Fontana, Bernini, and Borromini under Popes Paul V, Urban VIII and Innocent X. A new naturalistic chiaroscuro begins with the great painter Caravaggio, while the so-called eclectic painters of the school of Bologna—the Caracci, Domenichino, Guido Reni, and Guercino—endeavored to carry forward the classical tradition of Raphael.

Until the beginning of the 16th century, Roman music was in the hands of Netherlanders and Germans. But with the great masters Palestrina and Vittoria (the latter of Spanish origin) there begins the Roman tradition of music in church, theater, and concert hall, which leads to Carissimi and Pergolesi of the Neapolitan school.

The present aspect of Rome is essentially a creation of the Baroque. In the 17th century Rome became the artistic center of all Europe. Here the Fleming P. P. Rubens painted his pictures, here the Spaniard Velasquez portrayed Pope Innocent X, here the French Nicholas Poussin and the Alsatian Claude Lorrain conceived their magnificent landscapes, here worked the German Elsheimer. Baroque dominated Rome until well into the 18th century; the influence of Rococo was slight.

The new trend, running counter to Baroque, was Classicism, which received a great impetus from the discoveries and excavations at Herculaneum and Pompeii and gave rise to an enthusiastic preoccupation with ancient art. Clement XIV and Pius VI enriched their collections of ancient sculpture handed down from the Renaissance and built the Vatican Museum (p. 49) to house them. Canova, the greatest Classicist sculptor, worked in Rome. Upon the order of Napoleon the Piazza del Popolo and the Ascent of the Pincio were transformed in the Classicist spirit by Valadier (p. 113).

Classicism was the predominant trend until late in the

19th century. To it is due the preservation of ancient structures such as the Colosseum, which had been plundered for their own works by the great builders of the Renaissance and the Baroque. The scientific labors of archeology and modern art history begin. The Roman Forum, which still served as a pasture at the beginning of the 19th century, was gradually excavated.

Papal rule in Rome, uninterrupted since the Renaissance, was again broken in the revolutionary age of the ending 18th and the beginning 19th centuries. The revolutionary French armies invaded Rome in 1799 and declared it a Republic. Napoleon I incorporated the Papal States into his Empire, and designated his only son King of Rome. Twice, Popes were carried off to France as prisoners. After Napoleon's fall, Pius VII returned to the Vatican; but Italy's aspirations for national unity were more powerful than the Pope. After having united the greater part of Italy under his rule, King Victor Emmanuel II of Sardinia became King of Italy in 1861, and the parliament in Turin declared Rome the capital of the Kingdom of Italy. However, it was more than nine years later, that the King was able to take possession of Rome, when, on September 20, 1870, Italian troops entered the city after having breached the ancient Aurelian Wall near Porta Pia. The conquest of Rome ended the temporal power of the Pope which was restored only in 1929, when the Italian Government and the Holy See solved their disagreement on the "Roman Question" by the Lateran Treaty, establishing the independent sovereign State of Vatican City.

After 1870 began the great transformation of Rome into a modern metropolis. Parts of the old town were removed to make way for the regularization of the Tiber and the construction of new streets. The city extended into new quarters, the population growing from 208,000 in 1870 to 460,000 in 1901 and to more than 1½ million in 1947.

ROMAN FORUM—IMPERIAL FORA
COLOSSEUM—PALATINE

THE Latin word forum signifies "out of door." Hence the *Forum* was originally the site outside the villages built on the hills of Rome. It was a marshy lowland at the foot of the Palatine and Capitoline hills. In the regal period this area was drained and became a market and meeting place. Here peasants met to barter their produce. Later, the markets for cattle, vegetables, and fish were removed from the Forum, but booths of moneychangers, bankers, and goldsmiths were located in the Forum even in historical times.

In this market place the people first assembled to take counsel on common political, economic, and social questions. From these modest beginnings the Forum developed, with the rise of Rome, into the seat of political decisions of the highest importance, not for Italy alone, but for the whole world. In its *Curia* (senate house) or in the temples round about, the Roman Senate decreed war and peace. Upon its *rostra* (speaker's platform) sat Julius Caesar when Antony offered him the royal diadem, and from here Emperor Augustus in person determined litigation. By its *Lacus Curtius* Emperor Galba was cut down by rebellious soldiery in 69 B.C.; by its *Temple of Saturn* legionaries assassinated Emperor Vitellius. Through it leads the *Sacred Way* along which triumphators ascended to the *Temple of Jupiter Capitolinus,* with their trains of booty. In its *Tullianum,* the state prison, near the *Arch of Septimius Severus,* were imprisoned Rome's vanquished enemies, King Jugurtha of Numidia and Vercingetorix, the Gallic chief Julius Caesar led in triumph, and also, ac-

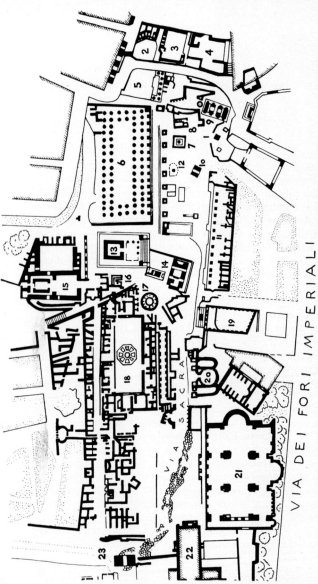

1. Lapis Niger—2. Portico dei Dei Consentes—3. Temple of Vespasian—4. Temple of Concordia—5. Temple of Saturn—6. Basilica Julia—7. Column of Phocas—8. Rostra—9. Arch of Septimius Severus—10. Anaglyphs of Trajan—11. Basilica Aemilia—12. Lacus Curtius—13. Temple of Castor—14. Temple of Divus Julius—15. Church of S. Maria Antiqua—16. Spring of Juturna—17. Temple of Vesta—18. Atrium Vestae—19. Temple of Antoninus and Faustina—20. Temple of Romulus—21. Basilica of Constantine—

VIA DEI FORI IMPERIALI

VIA SACRA

ROMAN FORUM. VIEW TOWARD THE ARCH OF TITUS

cording to tradition, the Apostle Peter. Every stone of the Roman Forum is drenched in blood. And it was here, in the Roman Forum, that the political forms of the Western World were created.

Even in the Renaissance the buildings of the Forum were much better preserved than they are today. The visitor must invoke his imagination to assist in deciphering the melancholy ruins. Many parts of the marble temples were gilded and painted. The Forum was filled with portrait statues of Roman statesmen. When the Roman Forum proved too small for the tumultuous political life at the end of the Republic, Julius Caesar built his own Forum adjoining it; and other great emperors, Augustus, Nerva, and Trajan, followed his example.

The Forum is reached by way of the Via dei Fori Imperiali near the Temple of Antoninus Pius and Faustina. For a general view we take a position near the modern tin roof which covers the *lapis niger*, a square of black marble blocks, and its underlying excavations, (see be-

ROMAN FORUM. VIEW TOWARD THE PALATINE

low). At a distance on our right we see the gleaming white Arch of Titus. To the right rises the Palatine Hill. Between the northern declivity of the Palatine and the southern declivity of the Capitoline with its Tarpeian Rock, from which Roman state criminals were hurled, a valley leads to the Tiber. The recently excavated road ascending the Palatine is the final portion of the Sacred Way.

Behind us, and facing away from us, the Palazzo del Senatore, on the Piazza Capitolina, rises sharply from the Forum. Its lower portion is part of the Roman *Tabularium,* the oldest structure in Rome still in use, built by the Consul Q. Lutatius Catulus in 78 B.C. In it were preserved state documents inscribed on bronze. The travertine structure opens to the Forum through an arched gallery with Doric half-columns. In the left-hand angle beneath the Tabularium stands the Corinthian *Porticus of the*

Dei Consentes, the twelve ancient gods of Rome. An inscription over the portico tells us that the City Prefect Vettius Praetextatus restored their statues in 367 A.D., clearly as a demonstration against Christianity.

Nearby rise the three handsome Corinthian columns of the *Temple of Vespasian,* the deified Emperor. The porch of this structure had six front columns; those remaining formed the right corner. The word *(r)estituer* in the inscription indicates that the temple was restored under Emperor Septimius Severus at the end of the 2nd century A.D.

To the right of the Temple of Vespasian stood the spacious *Temple of Concord.* Only a remnant of its base survives. A fragment of its elegant architrave is preserved in the vaults of the Tabularium (p. 121). This Temple of Concord was first planned by the dictator Furius Camillus, the conqueror of Veii, who thus celebrated the restored harmony between patricians and plebeians in 367 B.C. The remains derive from the structure which Tiberius dedicated in 10 A.D.

The eight columns on the lofty podium this side of the Sacred Way belong to the *Temple of Saturn,* of which they formed the porch. This temple was first built in 498 B.C., but the present ruins, with the inscription on the architrave, "The Senate and the Roman people have restored the temple destroyed by fire," belong to a late reconstruction, made perhaps at the beginning of the 5th century A.D. Saturn was god of agriculture, and his joyous festival was celebrated on December 17, at the end of the winter sowing. Presents were exchanged, and slaves dined at table with their masters.

Next to the Temple of Saturn stood the *Basilica Julia.* It contained a central hall measuring 269 x 59 ft., and four law courts, in which joint sessions were held. From its roof Emperor Caligula threw money to the people for his amusement. In the Renaissance the basilica belonged to a hospital which used it as a quarry and sold its blocks of marble and travertine.

In front of the Basilica Julia a tall fluted Corinthian

COLUMN OF PHOCAS

column, deriving from some unknown temple, rises from a base of brick masonry. In 608 A.D. the Byzantine governor of Italy, Smaragdus, erected upon it a gilded statue to the Byzantine Emperor Phocas. From this we know that the Forum still retained its public character up to that date. The *Column of Phocas* is its last historical monument.

Immediately adjoining our vantage point is the *rostra* (speaker's platform) which has been reconstructed in modern times. The name signifies "ships' beaks," commemorating the naval trophies affixed to it. Upon it stood statues of Sulla, Pompey, Julius Caesar, the youthful Augustus, and later emperors. From it were delivered formal harangues and eulogies of the great, at whose funerals their ancestors were impersonated, appropriately costumed and masked. The rostra as we see it does not date from the great days of the Republic, but is a later structure erected by Julius Caesar and the emperors.

In the pavement near the Column of Phocas there is a partly legible inscription, originally inlaid in large bronze letters: L. NAEVIUS . . . INU. S. PR. This refers to the Praetor Naevius Surdinus, who provided the Forum with a new travertine pavement in the time of Augustus. The pavement of the older portions of the Forum was some 6 ft. lower.

To study the early history of the Forum, we now examine the excavations under the modern tin roof we have chosen for our vantage point. Here the square of black marble blocks rises appreciably from the travertine pavement surrounding it. Roman writers record that the grave of Romulus, the mythical founder of Rome, lay under the *lapis niger,* "black stone," and accordingly the Roman archeologist Jacopo Boni began his excavations at this point in 1899. Descending the stairs under the tin roof, we find his discovery: two stone bases of Etruscan form which once bore the figures of recumbent lions. These probably formed part of a chapel that rose behind them. There is also a four-sided upright stele (inscribed stone) upon which are visible traces of a Latin inscription. The Latin is so ancient that it has defied interpretation, but it certainly contains the word king *(rex)*. The monument must therefore belong to the regal period, and the inscription probably has to do with religious prescriptions. These remains date from approximately 600 B.C.

The area between the *lapis niger,* the Arch of Septimius Severus, and the Curia was occupied by the ancient republican *Comitium,* the place of political assembly of the Roman people, which contained the ancient rostra, and a pulpit for emissaries from foreign states. Here was enacted the important role of Rome before the Forum was transformed by Julius Caesar.

We now consider the *Arch of Septimius Severus.* This arch, that of Titus, and that of Constantine, are not in fact triumphal arches as they are erroneously called. The pavement of the central span of the Arch of Severus is so high that no triumphal chariot could pass it. Rather are these Roman arched portals motivated by the same ancient religious sentiment as is the opening of the holy door at St. Peter's and other great basilicas of Rome in a

DECENNIAL BASE OF DIOCLETIAN

jubilee year: By passing through the sacred portal, the
devotee rids himself of his guilt. This ancient religious
concept is here connected with another, derived from the
Hellenistic art of Greece: the honorific monument erected
upon a lofty substructure, to be seen far and wide.

The inscription on the pediment of the arch, originally
in gilt bronze letters, tells us that it was erected in 203
A.D. by the Senate and the Roman people to Emperor
Septimius Severus and his sons Geta and Caracalla, for
preserving the State and extending the Empire. After
Caracalla murdered his brother, the latter's name was
effaced and replaced by symbolic titles. The reliefs on
the bases of the columns show Roman soldiers leading
oriental captives. The spandrels of the arch have Victories with their trophies. Below are small figures of the
Seasons—Winter and Spring on the Forum side, Summer
and Autumn on the Capitoline side—as symbols of pros-

ANAGLYPH OF TRAJAN

perity under the reign of the Emperor. The reliefs over
the smaller arches, executed in a magnificent and novel
style, illustrate the prowess of the Emperor in his war
against his rival Pescennius Niger, and his conquest of
Mesopotamia. Surmounting the arch was a bronze group
showing the Emperor and his sons in a chariot drawn by
six horses.

Close to the arch, upon a high modern pedestal, is the
decennial base of Emperor Diocletian, erected in 303 A.D.,
in honor of his thirty-year reign. The principal scene shows
the Emperor, his head veiled, offering sacrifice, while
Victory flies toward him to crown him with a garland.
Also shown are Mars, the god of war, to whom the sacrifice is offered, the seated goddess Roma, and the Genius
of the Roman Senate. The other faces show a procession
of Roman citizens and officers and also the sacrificial animals, boar, ram, and bull, sacred to Mars. On the remaining face, figures of Victory hold a triumphal shield
bearing the inscription *Caesarum decennalia feliciter*,

"Felicitations for the ten-year jubilee of the reign of the Caesars" (Diocletian and his three co-regents).

The *Curia Julia,* on the east side of this part of the Forum, is a late structure, dating from 303 A.D. (The previous senate houses were burnt and rebuilt several times.) The present building was preserved almost intact because, in the 7th century, Pope Honorius transformed it into a church. Recently it has been restored to its ancient form. Its outer wall still shows, near the top, remains of the original painted stucco facing, and its interior preserves portions of the colorful marble pavement, and shows the arrangement of the senators' benches, the niches for the images of the gods, and by the remains of its base, the location of the statue of Victoria, brought from Tarentum by Augustus, as a symbol of Roman world dominion. It was removed in 357 A.D., upon the demand of the Christians, but returned to its place by the Emperor Julian the Apostate, who favored paganism. Dispute over the statue broke out again under the youthful Emperor Valentinian II. The leader of the pagan party was the rich and cultivated Senator Symmachus, and his opponent was Ambrose, the great bishop of Milan, and teacher of Saint Augustine. The Christians prevailed and Victoria was banished.

Inside the Curia are now to be found the so-called *Anaglyphs of Trajan,* which were formerly wrongly thought to be parts of the rostra, and stood in the central space of the Forum. These are two marble screens decorated on both sides with reliefs. Since, like the decennial base dedicated to Mars, they show the sacrificial animals sacred to that deity, these stones must also relate to the god of war. The other reliefs on one screen show the Emperor addressing the populace from the rostra, and in the background the buildings of the Forum. Behind the throng is a seated statue, and beside it a female deity with child in arms; this is the *Pietas Augusti,* the symbol of the Emperor's clemency. The other screen again shows the Emperor upon the rostra with the buildings of the Forum in the background. Before him a group of officials are

TEMPLE OF ANTONINUS AND FAUSTINA

bringing tablets and placing them in two piles, probably records of debts to be destroyed. Both panels present social measures of the Emperor Trajan, such as foundations for orphans and cancellations of indebtedness.

The long structure which extends from the Curia to the entrance of the Forum is the ruin of the *Basilica Aemilia*. The Aemilii belonged to Rome's oldest and most distinguished nobility. In 187 B.C. the Consul M. Aemilius Lepidus built the Via Aemilia which continued the Via Flaminia from Rimini through Bologna to Piacenza. This road has given its name to the modern Italian province of Emilia. Later the Via Aemilia was continued to Nice. The Basilica Aemilia was built and several times restored by members of the Aemilii family. In 14 B.C. the Basilica was destroyed by fire, and later rebuilt by Augustus. It was a two-storied, arched structure. Some few stones of the façade of the ancient edifice, decorated with ox skulls and sacrificial vessels executed in the finest Augustan style, are preserved. Augustus' building was also burnt, apparently in Alaric's invasion of 410 A.D., and was restored by Emperor Honorius.

At the left of the entrance to the Forum, built into a wall, is an inscription recomposed from fragments. It records, in beautiful, monumental script, that the Senate had erected to Lucius Caesar, son of the deified Augustus, the building from which the inscription derived.

Opposite the Basilica Aemilia, near the Column of Phocas, is a circular area enclosed by a fence, its center covered with a metal sheet. This is the *Lacus Curtius*. According to Roman legend a deep cleft in the earth appeared here 362 B.C., and an oracle proclaimed that it would close only if Rome sacrificed to it her most precious possession. A noble youth named Marcus Curtius interpreted this as signifying weapons and courage, and flung himself into the abyss, which thereupon closed. This deed is portrayed on a Roman relief in the Museo Nuovo on the Capitoline Hill.

Sunk into the Forum pavement nearby is the pedestal, in three blocks, for a prancing bronze steed that once stood upon it. This belonged to the colossal equestrian statue of the Emperor Domitian, erected to commemorate his victory over the Germans in 91 A.D.

The *Temple of Castor* is the last of the great buildings on the west side of the Forum. Worship of Castor and Pollux, twin sons of Zeus, was native to Sparta, whence they came to southern Italy with the Spartan emigrants who founded Tarentum. As part of the great influence which Greek religion exercised upon Roman, these gods were worshiped in Rome also. A legend arose that they had assisted the Roman people at Lake Regillus in 499 B.C. in the last battle against the ousted royal house of the Tarquins, had determined the victory, had brought tidings of it to Rome, and had watered their horses at a spring in the Forum. The origins of the temple are surely very ancient, but its remains derive from a reconstruction of Tiberius in 6 A.D. A cella (the enclosed space of a temple) surrounded by a double colonnade of 11 columns each stood upon a lofty podium. The three surviving Corinthian columns are 39 ft. high. Beautiful fragments of the architrave lie at the west of the temple.

The large brick structure on the declivity of the Palatine Hill belongs to the *Temple of Divus Augustus,* which was begun by Tiberius, dedicated by Caligula, and restored in 88 A.D. by Domitian after a fire. After the 6th century A.D., Greek monks built the *Church of S. Maria Antiqua* in a portion of this structure and decorated it richly with frescoes. In the left aisle are pictures from the Old Testament, the story of Joseph being the best preserved. Near the entrance of the ascent to the Palatine is an early Christian sarcophagus, on which Jonah, spewed forth from the whale, is shown resting under a gourd. The center shows a man reading and a woman praying. Then come the Good Shepherd and Christ's Baptism in the Jordan. The choir, reached from the central nave by three steps, has a fresco on its right-hand inner side showing the ailing King Hezekiah in bed and the prophet Isaiah foretelling his death. In the presbytery, at the extreme upper left, an Adoration of the Magi, and, beneath it, Christ Bearing His Cross. In the semicircular apse there are several registers of frescoes, the uppermost showing Christ surrounded by six-winged cherubim presenting Pope Paul I to the Virgin. The chapel left of the presbytery contains the best-preserved frescoes. Above the altar is a crucifixion with Mary, John, and Longinus. On the side walls are the stories of Saints Quiricus and Gulitta, who suffered martyrdom at Tarsus, in Cilicia. In the 9th century the ruins of the Palatine threatened to crush the Church of S. Maria Antiqua, and Pope Leo IV moved it to the Temple of Venus and Rome, where it was called S. Maria Nuova (now S. Francesca Romana).

Returning to the Forum, we find opposite us, to the right of the Temple of Castor, the *Spring of Juturna,* a basin 16¼ ft. deep. Juturna was a water deity, and it was here that legend had Castor and Pollux water their horses. The reliefs on the altar near the basin show Castor and Pollux with their horses, their mother Leda with the swan,

Jupiter, their father, and a goddess of light with a torch, probably their sister Helen. Near the basin of Juturna we get a view of a small chapel with a statue of Aesculapius, the Greek god of healing. At his side, an acolyte carries the cock, which was the god's favorite animal. Further to the right, in front of a small Chapel of Juturna, there is a handsome, circular well-curb of Augustan style, bearing the dedicatory inscription of M. Barbatius Pollio, apparently a political friend of Antony.

Adjoining the Chapel of Juturna to the right is a hall which was transformed in Christian times into an *Oratory of the Forty Martyrs*. The martyrs are represented, slowly freezing in an icy pond, on the large fresco of the apse. On the lower wall to the left, near the apse, are two large Latin crosses with medallions at their center and with pendant crowns.

We proceed further on our return to the Forum and find the *Temple of Vesta* at our right. This was partially reconstructed in 1930, travertine supplementing the ancient marble remains. The lofty podium has protruding bases upon which twenty Corinthian columns, originally joined by metal trellis work, surround a circular cella. The frieze relief exhibits sacrificial vessels and priestly symbols. The ancient remains date from the reconstruction of Julia Domna, wife of Emperor Septimius Severus.

The circular structure is modeled upon the round huts of ancient Italy such as may still be seen in the Roman Campagna, the walls woven of reeds and covered with a thatched roof. Vesta is the ancient Latin deity of the hearth and the home, and, by analogy, of the state's hearth. The fire in the Temple of Vesta, tended by six Vestals bound to chastity during their term of service, was never permitted to go out. The temple contained the relics upon which Rome's welfare depended.

Behind the Temple of Vesta is the *Atrium Vestae* which contained offices and living quarters for the college of six Vestals. These were selected for their rigorous duties as children between six and ten, originally from highly distinguished families, and were given extraordinary privi-

TEMPLE OF ROMULUS

leges. The extant remains of the atrium go back largely
to Emperor Septimius Severus. Statues of the chief Vestals
in official dress decorate the court. A marble base near
the exit shows an inscription of 364 A.D. for the statue
of a Vestal who is particularly praised for her "chastity
and expertness in sacrifice and sacred usages." Her name,
however, had been erased as a mark of disgrace, and this
has given rise to the conjecture that she was the Vestal
Claudia, of whom the poet Prudentius relates that she
entered the Convent of San Lorenzo as a Christian.

Opposite the Temple of Vesta, close to the Temple of
Castor, are the foundations of the *Arch of Augustus*. It
had three bays, and was erected in 19 B.C. to commemorate the Parthians' return of the military standards lost to

them by Crassus. The east side of the arch touches the *Temple of Divus Julius*, the deified Julius Caesar. After his assassination on the Ides of March in 44 B.C., his friends brought his body to the Forum. Here Antony delivered a eulogy of Caesar (represented in Act III of Shakespeare's *Julius Caesar*), and the corpse was cremated on a hastily improvised pyre. In 42 B.C. the Triumvirs Octavius, Antony, and Lepidus erected upon the spot a temple, and a statue of Julius Caesar with a star over his head as a symbol of his immortality. The temple rose from a podium which, like the large rostra, was decorated with ships' beaks. The larger portion of the reconstructed podium is modern. Its niche contains a circular altar, probably at the spot of the pyre.

Behind this structure, architectural fragments of various dates lie upon the ground. These belong to the *Regia*, which, according to Roman tradition, was the house of the king, who was the state's religious as well as political representative. After the fall of the monarchy, the chief priest, the Pontifex Maximus, succeeded to this structure, which was his official seat. He arranged the calendar of the annual religious festivals, and his chronicles of the year's events, political officials, religious prodigies, and the like, constituted the beginnings of Roman historiography. Here too was the Chapel of Mars with his sacred spears, which clashed when war was imminent. Another chapel was sacred to Ops, the goddess of rich harvest. Only the Pontifex Maximus and the Vestals had access to it.

Opposite the Regia the *Temple of Antoninus and Faustina* stands upon a lofty podium; in the Middle Ages this structure was transformed into the Church of S. Lorenzo in Miranda. Six columns of the porch of cipollino (onion stone) with marble capitals are preserved. At the center of the broad stairway are the remains of the ancient altar. According to the lower line of the inscription on the architrave, Emperor Antoninus Pius erected the temple to the memory of his wife, the elder Faustina, who died in 141 A.D. After the Emperor's death the temple was dedicated to him also and the upper line of the inscrip-

FORUM OF JULIUS CAESAR

tion was added. The frieze of the temple exhibits winged griffins guarding sacred trees, and candelabra with sacred fire.

At the southern corner of the temple a modern tin roof shelters an ancient cemetery, the so-called *Sepolcretum*, which was uncovered in 1902 at a depth of 20 ft. Its older graves, which go back to the 9th century B.C., belong to the period in which the deceased were cremated and their remains deposited in cinerary urns of black or dark-brown clay in the shape of huts. In the later graves, which go back to the 6th century B.C., the deceased were not cremated, but laid to rest in wooden coffins. Finds from the Sepolcretum are preserved in the Forum Museum, in a building formerly a monastery, adjacent to the Church of S. Francesca Romana.

As we proceed along the Sacred Way, we find at our left a dainty circular building which was surmounted by a lantern in the 17th century. This building has kept not

27

only its ancient doorway but even the original bronze door in which the mechanism of the ancient lock still operates. For a long while the structure was thought to be the *Memorial Temple of Romulus,* erected in 307 A.D. by Emperor Maxentius in honor of his son. Probably it was only the lateral entrance hall to the Temple of the Penates in Vespasian's Forum of Peace, which lay behind it.

We turn back and leave the Forum at the Temple of Antoninus and Faustina to inspect the *Imperial Fora* along the Via dei Fori Imperiali. The oldest of these is the *Forum of Julius Caesar,* which begins immediately behind the Curia of the Senate. In order to relieve the crowding of the old Forum, Julius Caesar planned an extension at his own expense. At the decisive Battle of Pharsalus he vowed a temple to Venus, the mythical ancestress of his house. It was built in his Forum and dedicated in 46 B.C. In it he set up a golden statue of Queen Cleopatra of Egypt.

The Forum is in the shape of an elongated rectangle, with a double colonnade for shops. The temple at the short northern end was surrounded upon three sides by a colonnade of closely placed Corinthian columns, with eight in front. Extant portions of the structure, with fragments of the cella frieze showing Cupids slaughtering sacrificial victims and carrying vessels for the cult of Venus, do not belong to Caesar's structure, but to a reconstruction of Domitian which was dedicated by Trajan in 113 A.D. The axis of the Forum of Caesar was imitated in the axes of the succeeding fora.

Opposite the Forum of Caesar, across the street, is the *Forum of Augustus.* At the Battle of Philippi in 42 B.C., in which Augustus defeated the party of the assassinators of Caesar, he vowed a temple to Mars Ultor, "the avenging Mars," and dedicated it in 2 B.C. The plan of his Forum is similar to that of the Forum of Caesar. The temple and its colonnade, in front of which remains of the ancient altar are still visible, dominates the long rectangular space, which is enlarged at the sides by great semicircular apses. In the niches of the apses and colon-

FORUM OF AUGUSTUS

nade stood the statues of the mythical ancestors of Augustus and of the great men of Roman history in the age of the Republic. At the end of the colonnade to the left of the temple stood a marble statue of Augustus seven times life size, or 39 ft. high.

The Temple of Mars was protected from the constant danger of fire in the crowded quarter by a circuit wall of peperino (volcanic rock) over 100 ft. high. A large portion of this wall still exists, accessible from the Via Tor di Conti, and is one of the most imposing sights of Rome. The Gothic embrasure over the left apse of the Forum of Augustus and the delicately arched Renaissance gallery high above the street belong to the palace of the Order of the Maltese Cross, which occupied this space in the Middle Ages.

Adjacent to the Forum of Augustus at the left is the *Forum of Trajan*, dedicated in 113 A.D. It surpassed its predecessors in size and magnificence. Its architect was

Apollodorus of Damascus. With its Column of Trajan, and the Temple of the deified Trajan, as yet unexcavated, which was built at its rear by Emperor Hadrian, this Forum was a magnificent structural composition. It was entered from the Forum of Augustus, through a triumphal arch surmounted by a bronze group: Trajan standing in a triumphal chariot drawn by six horses. In the center of the great pillared court, which had large lateral apses like its model, the Forum of Augustus, stood an equestrian statue of Trajan. From the court, three portals opened into the Basilica Ulpia, a magnificent hall 82 ft. wide and 426 ft. long, with apses at its longitudinal axis, the whole being supported by ninety-six columns of porphyry.

Behind this basilica rises the *Column of Trajan* to its original height of 88 ft. Trajan was buried in the base of the column. The column consists of seventeen huge drums of Parian marble. Its interior contains a spiral stairway of 185 steps. The column was surmounted by a bronze statue of Trajan; the present statue of St. Peter was set up by Pope Sixtus V. The spiral relief which coils about the shaft is over 660 ft. long and contains about 2500 human figures. With a wealth of magnificent compositions, the reliefs depict the chief events in Trajan's two wars against the Dacians. On a clear day they may be studied with the naked eye. Our surroundings recall a medieval legend of Pope Gregory the Great: During a procession he was so moved by the beauty of this Forum that he offered prayers for its builder and so redeemed him from hell-fire.

Retracing our steps we arrive behind the apse of the Forum. Separated from it by a wall and a street which retains its original pavement, there rises, in six stories, the *Market of Trajan*. This was freed from the later additions in excavations undertaken after 1926. The building served the administration of the Imperial treasury for distribution of provisions to the poorer populace. The modern visitor enters it behind the Forum and ascends by an astonishingly well-preserved staircase into a large hall (in which expositions are now held), and at its upper

MARKET OF TRAJAN

level finally emerges on the Via del IV Novembre near the medieval tower, the Torre delle Milizie.

We pass the Forum of Augustus and reach at its right the remains of the *Forum of Nerva* (actually a construction of Emperor Domitian). This is a long and narrow strip beginning at the right apse of the Forum of Augustus and ending near the Basilica Aemilia in the Forum Romanum. Its small *Temple of Minerva* was demolished by Pope Paul V in 1606 for the sake of its building stone. Only two columns with their architrave and a portion of the sculptured frieze from the southeastern wall of the Forum are preserved. The frieze tells the story of Arachne of Lydia, who boasted that she surpassed the goddess Athene in the art of weaving and whom the deity punished by turning her into a spider.

Adjoining the Forum of Nerva were the Forum of

Vespasian and the Temple of Peace, which have not yet been excavated.

We proceed along the busy Via dei Fori Imperiali by the Church of SS. Cosma e Damiano, to the *Basilica of Constantine;* (three modern maps of the history of the Roman Empire are attached to its exterior wall). The basilica was begun by Emperor Maxentius, and completed

FORUM OF NERVA

by Constantine in 312 A.D. Its gigantic brick masonry covered an area of 64,500 sq. ft. It consisted of two aisles and a central nave. Only the northern aisle, with its three huge coffered vaults, is still erect. A corresponding southerly aisle has collapsed. The nave rose to a height of 115 ft. One of the Corinthian columns which probably supported the nave now stands in front of S. Maria Maggiore, bearing a statue of the Virgin. In the central bay, which

COLOSSEUM

now serves for summer concerts of classical music, Constantine instituted a court of law. He placed a colossal portrait of himself in the central apse of the nave. This statue was of wood with head and limbs in marble; the latter are now in the court of the Palazzo dei Conservatori (p. 146). The huge vaults of this basilica, even more grandiose than the vaulted construction of the Baths of Caracalla (p. 93) and of Diocletian (p. 136), represent the last great achievement of Roman architecture. This style was continued in Hagia Sophia at Constantinople, St. Peter's in Rome, and still survives in the great vaulted structures of modern buildings.

We leave the basilica and follow the street to the *Colosseum*. This great structure for gladiatorial combats, beast hunts, and similar spectacles, was built by Emperor Vespasian in 72 A.D. to conciliate the populace after the excesses of Nero, on the site of an artificial lake which belonged to the Golden House of Nero (p. 34). Its exterior was planned in three superimposed orders—Doric, Ionic, and Corinthian respectively. The labor was supplied by captives brought from Judaea after the fall of Jeru-

33

salem (70 A.D.), and contemporaries marveled that the stone facing dressed the upper part of the concrete core before the lower walls were finished. Titus added a fourth story (not included in the original plan) in 80 A.D. On the wall between the windows of the fourth floor were hung large round shields of bronze. Above were consoles for the wooden masts which carried a great awning to shield spectators from the sun. Statues were set up in the arcades of the second and third stories. A cleverly designed system of broad stairways leads from the ground-floor galleries to the rows of seats on the several stories, and permitted the amphitheater to be emptied rapidly. There were seats for some 50,000 people. The interior of the arena contained complicated subterranean structures for the animals used in the spectacles. At the games presented by Emperor Philip the Arab in 249 A.D., one thousand pairs of gladiators, thirty-two elephants, sixty lions, ten giraffes, and six hippopotamuses were shown. The stones of the Colosseum provided the Popes with building material for a number of palaces and churches, until the retaining walls ordered by Popes Gregory XVI and Pius IX in the 19th century put a halt to the destruction.

Ascending through the parks of the Colle Oppio, north of the Colosseum, we reach the *Golden House of Nero*. This was not merely a palace, but a huge complex of parks and gardens extending from the Palatine and the Roman Forum immediately to the rear of the Regia to the declivity of the Esquiline, and embracing the entire area of the Colosseum, the Arch of Constantine, and the adjacent region. It contained wheat fields, vineyards, corrals for animals wild and tame, an artificial lake at the present site of the Colosseum, and, near the present Church of S. Francesca Romana, a colossal bronze statue of Nero some 98 ft. tall. The expense of these vast pleasure grounds bankrupted not only the Emperor but also the Empire. At Nero's death (68 A.D.) the highly unpopular project had not yet been completed; Emperor Vespasian halted the work and built the Colosseum instead. Later

ARCH OF CONSTANTINE

Nero's palaces on the Palatine and the Esquiline were destroyed by fire. Trajan built on the site of the Golden House his Baths, the remains of which are to be found in the parks mentioned above. The interior of the Golden House contained a circular dining hall which revolved as the earth revolves; it also had dining rooms with movable ceilings of ivory from which flowers and perfumes were sprayed upon the diners. The numerous rooms which are preserved present an ill-assorted mixture of excessively high-ceilinged corridors, rooms, and large halls, badly illuminated and hard to heat. The rich paintings of the ceilings are largely contemporary with those of Pompeii and executed in a kindred style. Their ornate motifs take no account of the fact that distance would make them invisible to the viewer.

We retrace our steps past the Colosseum and reach the *Arch of Constantine*. The inscription on its pediment informs us that the Roman Senate had resolved upon its erection in 312 A.D., to commemorate Constantine's victory over Emperor Maxentius. The arch itself is a homogeneous structure, but many of its decorative elements were taken from buildings of earlier emperors. The figures of Dacians in Phrygian marble, the reliefs on the short ends of the pediment, and the related reliefs on the side walls of the central arch were taken from a monument of Emperor Trajan. The medallions over the lateral bays, showing hunting scenes, belonged to a structure of Emperor Hadrian. The reliefs at either side of the pediment inscription decorated a triumphal arch of Emperor Marcus Aurelius. Only the reliefs on the base, showing Roman soldiers, northern captives, and Victories, as well as the small friezes over the side arches, belong to the period of Constantine. Of especial interest are the friezes of the south side. That over the left arch shows Constantine's siege of Verona in 312 A.D.; that over the right arch, the battle at the Milvian Bridge, in the same year. The walls of the central arch show first Emperor Trajan addressing his army while Victoria descends to crown him. The relief opposite shows the Emperor and his guard pressing against vanquished Dacians.

As we return to the Roman Forum, ascending the Sacred Way to the Arch of Titus, we have on our right the double *Temple of Venus and Rome.* The two apses, of which the eastern one contained a colossal image of Venus, and the western one of Rome, were set back to back. The cella was surrounded by a Corinthian colonnade, with ten columns in front. On the Colosseum side granite colonnades, some of the columns of which have been set upright again, formed an open court. The temple was dedicated by Hadrian in 1936 A.D. and restored by Maxentius. The northern portion is now occupied by the Church of S. Francesca Romana.

The *Arch of Titus* was dedicated, according to the pediment inscription on its south side, to the deified Titus; it was erected by Domitian in 81 A.D. In the Middle Ages it became incorporated into the fortress of the Frangipani family and as a result was partly destroyed; the French architect Valadier reconstructed the

ARCH OF TITUS

north side in 1821. Unlike the triple arches of Septimius Severus and Constantine, the Arch of Titus has only one bay, and whereas the columns of the former are free-standing, here we have three-quarter columns. At the center of the coffered ceiling, a relief shows Titus borne to heaven by an eagle. The right wall represents Titus' triumphal procession after the conquest of Jerusalem in 70 A.D., the booty consisting of the seven-branched candelabrum, the table of show-bread, and the sacred trumpets. On the opposite side Titus, crowned by a Victory and accompanied by lictors, stands in a triumphal chariot drawn by four horses.

Beyond the Arch of Titus a broad road leads to the

Palatine Hill. (This may also be reached from the Temple of Augustus or by a path behind the Temple of Vesta.)

The Palatine owes its present appearance as a flat terrace to the building activities of the emperors, and in particular of Nero and Domitian. The extensive destruction of the classical monuments is to be explained by the fact that in the Middle Ages Roman nobles built their castles, with numerous towers, in the ruins of the ancient buildings.

We ascend the road to the Palatine; then, after a short distance, turn to the right and mount the steps to the charming *Casino Farnese,* the remains of the gardens of the Farnese family. This family undertook the earliest large-scale excavations of ancient statuary on the Palatine, in the 16th century. The stairs at the right, alongside the Casino, take us to the Palatine terrace; walking along the flowered borders we reach the evergreen oaks and the magnificent view of the Forum. A few steps farther, along the side facing the Capitoline, we obtain a majestic view of the Tiber region as far as St. Peter's. Down a small stairway to the left we come to a small, deep-lying grove of evergreen oaks. Here stood the *Temple of the Great Mother,* first dedicated in 191 B.C. In front of the podium of the temple are remains of its architectural members and of the image of the seated goddess.

We pass a series of chambers belonging to the Palace of Tiberius, which has not yet been excavated, and arrive at a cistern vaulted by circular projecting blocks, dating from the late Republic.

Alongside it and some yards lower is a partially preserved house whose three principal rooms are decorated with fine paintings. The discovery of lead water pipes marked with the name of Livia, wife of Augustus, makes it likely that this house, now called the *House of Livia,* quite unprepossessing according to our notions, belonged to Augustus, the richest and most powerful man of his time. We descend to the vestibule with its mosaic pavement; from there straight ahead through a court into three adjoining rooms. The main painting—Io guarded by

PALATINE. FLAVIAN PALACE

Argus, with Mercury approaching to release her—is in the central room. On the right side of the court is the dining room. Because of its proximity to the Forum, and the cool summer breezes afforded by its elevation, the Palatine was the favored residential quarter of the Roman world. Cicero too had his house here.

To the left of the House of Livia, a subterranean passage leads to the ruins of the great *Flavian Palace* constructed by Domitian (81-96 A.D.). Its architect was Rabirius, friend of the poet Martial. The front portion of the palace, parts of the walls of which still stand erect, contained as its central hall a throne room measuring 148 by 118 ft., roofed by a barrel vault. Behind it was a large colonnade landscaped and fitted with a pool; its place is now occupied by the modern gardens. At the west are remains of a nymphaeum (garden room) where the water played over three steps. At the fenced-in spot where the pavement has collapsed, we get a view of the mighty supporting walls constructed by Nero for the portion of the Golden House which once stood at this place. Deep underneath are the remains of a fountain, fitted with niches and little columns, belonging to Nero's original palace which he later built over.

Abutting on the triclinium (dining hall) on the east is the newly excavated complex of the Palace of Augustus which took advantage of the slope of the hill; this is not yet accessible to the visitor.

Adjoining this is the so-called *Stadium of the Palatine*, the Hippodromus, covering an area of 525 by 157 ft., intended for formal gardens rather than for horse racing. It was surrounded with a colonnade topped by a gallery from which the gardens could be enjoyed. The large niche at the center was probably the emperor's loge. At the southern longitudinal side of the Hippodrome, behind the so-called emperor's loge, lie the ruins of the *Palace of Septimius Severus*, with the vaults of his Baths. The terrace, supported by the still extant substructures of the palace, affords a magnificent view. Below and to the left are the arches of the Claudian aqueduct which supplied the Palatine. In the left distance is the Lateran hill, with the group of churches of S. Gregorio Magno in the foreground. St. Gregory himself founded the Church of S. Gregorio Magno, with its Benedictine monastery, of which he was the superior, in 575. Nearby are the Chapels of S. Silvia (Gregory's mother), S. Andreas, and S. Barbara. Behind is the Church of S. Stefano Rotondo, a circular building of the 5th century (p. 92). To the right is the gigantic shell of Caracalla's Baths (p. 93). Behind this rises the round tomb of Caecilia Metella on the Via Appia (p. 98), dating from the middle of the 1st century B.C. Further to the right is the Pyramid of Cestius, built by the tribune and praetor, C. Cestius (p. 90) in 12 B.C. as his funeral monument. The gleaming white buildings in the distance, still incomplete, were planned by Mussolini for a world exposition. In the valley beneath lies ancient Rome's largest circus, the Circus Maximus, as yet unexcavated. It accommodated an audience of 80,000 for the beast hunts, and other spectacles of the Empire.

We now return, by the Sacred Way, passing the monastery of S. Bonaventura, to the exit from the Forum.

ST. PETER'S AND THE VATICAN PALACE

CROSSING the Tiber to St. Peter's by the Ponte Vittorio Emanuele, a magnificent view opens before us. On the right are the heights of the Pincio, with the two towers of the Church of Santissima Trinità dei Monti. On the river bank, to the right, tower the massive modern Palace of Justice, and the lofty circular structure of the Castel S. Angelo. Directly before us are the Hospital and Church of S. Spirito in Sassia, erected by Sixtus IV in the late 15th century, and the first glimpse of St. Peter's. On the left are the heights of the Janiculum with its beacon and the equestrian monument of Giuseppe Garibaldi. In the left foreground, this side of the river, is the Church of S. Giovanni dei Fiorentini, the national church of the Florentines, built in 1521.

On the right, the *Ponte S. Angelo* leads to the *Castel S. Angelo.* Its central arches were part of an ancient bridge built by Emperor Hadrian in A.D. 136. The statues of angels which decorate the bridge are from the workshop of Bernini. The Castel S. Angelo is a cylindrical structure like the Tomb of Caecilia Metella (p. 98) and the Mausoleum of Augustus (p. 107). Arising from a square base, it has a diameter of 210 ft. It was built by Emperor Hadrian as a burial place for himself and his family, and was completed by Emperor Antoninus Pius in A.D. 139. The interior contained the sepulchers of emperors from Hadrian to Caracalla. None of these are preserved. The present name of the structure derives from a legend according to which the archangel Michael, sheathing his sword, appeared to Pope Gregory the Great in 596 during a procession to avert the plague. The colossal bronze figure on the roof, representing the archangel, was executed by the Flemish sculptor Verschaffelt in 1752. As early as the Gothic incursions in the 6th century the Mausoleum was used as a place of refuge. The Popes transformed it into a fortress, with elegant living quarters and a state prison. To this fortress Clement VII fled when Rome was sacked by the mercenaries of Charles V. The interior is accessible as a public museum.

A view of *St. Peter's* opens through the new Via della Conciliazione. In front of the basilica spreads the *Piazza S. Pietro,* the most beautiful creation of its kind in the modern world. It is an oval adjoining a quadrangle, the ascent of which is crowned by St. Peter's. The design of the square and of the magnificent colonnades with their statues of saints, 162 in number, on the balustrade, are Bernini's. There are four rows of Doric columns, altogether 284. The construction dates from between 1655 and 1667, during the office of Pope Alexander VII. The square measures 372 by 262 yards.

The obelisk at the center, from Heliopolis in Egypt, is 82 ft. high, and was taken from the Circus of Caligula. Of the two splendid fountains whose perpetual rippling spray overflows their basins, that nearer the Vatican was constructed by Maderna in 1613, and the other in 1675.

The Old St. Peter's, which preceded the present structure, was a foundation of Emperor Constantine in A.D. 326, erected as a memorial church over the tomb of the Apostle Peter. Recent excavations beneath its level, under the left aisle of the present church, have revealed an ancient Roman cemetery street of the 2nd to the 4th century, with sepulchral chapels decorated with paintings and stucco, some in a good state of preservation; these are accessible only by special permission. Old St. Peter's was a basilica of five aisles, richly decorated with pictures in mosaic.

When the millennium-old structure fell into disrepair, Julius II began the new structure of St. Peter's in 1506. The plans were designed by Bramante, who, as he put it,

CASTEL S. ANGELO

wished to superimpose the dome of the Pantheon (p. 76) upon the vaults of the Basilica of Constantine (p. 32). His design showed a Greek cross with equal arms, with a large central dome, to which four smaller domes with side chapels were adjoined. In 1547, after the death of Bramante, Michelangelo took over the direction of the building. He simplified and accentuated his predecessor's design by strengthening the piers which support the dome and subordinating the whole to the effect of the large central dome. Michelangelo's plan was largely executed, but suffered a fatal alteration under Pope Paul V, whose name figures on the façade of St. Peter's; he lengthened the nave in order to reproduce the dimensions of Old St. Peter's. The predominance of the magnificent dome was thus lost both for the front view and for the effect of the interior. The Baroque façade is by Maderna; from its central loggia the Pope imparts his benediction upon Rome and the world on Easter Sunday. The new church was consecrated by Urban VIII in 1626.

The portico with its elegant stucco ceiling has, on the left, a Baroque equestrian statue of Charlemagne. The bronze doors at the center are the work of the Florentine Filarete. Its central panels show St. Paul with sword and mystic vessel, and St. Peter with the Pope kneeling at his side. Beneath is the martyrdom of the two Apostles in Rome. The surrounding frieze shows figures from Greek and Roman mythology. The fifth door at the right is the *Porta Santa,* opened only on jubilee years, and otherwise walled up.

St. Peter's is the largest and most magnificent church in the world. Its dimensions are: area, 163,185 sq. ft.; diameter of dome, 138 ft.; height of dome, 436 ft. St. Peter's appears less appropriate to quiet individual worship than as a setting for the papal functions and their mystic meaning. The magnificent scheme of the structure becomes apparent in an unhurried promenade.

Immediately before us, on entering the nave, is a round slab of porphyry marking the spot where German kings were crowned as emperors of the Holy Roman Empire in Old St. Peter's; in the pavement, dimensions of the largest churches are given for comparison. By the fourth pillar to the right is the venerable seated bronze statue of St. Peter, dating from the 13th century, its right foot kissed by the devout. Nearby and surrounded by ever-burning lamps is the *confessio,* the entrance to the tomb of St. Peter. Below, the marble statue of Pius VI at prayer, by Canova.

The high altar is reserved exclusively for Masses celebrated by the Pope. Its four spiral columns with the canopy designed by Bernini in 1633 are cast of the bronze which roofed the porch of the Pantheon.

At the four piers which support the dome are the huge statues, over 15 ft. high, of St. Longinus with the Lance by Bernini, St. Helena with the Cross and its nails by Mocchi, St. Veronica with the Veil by Bolgi, and St. Andrew by Duquesnoy.

Near these statues stairs lead down to the so-called *Grottoes.* The new St. Peter's is 11 ft. above the preserved

ST. PETER'S

level of the Old, and the intervening space was filled
with chapels and sepulchral vaults. Here are numerous
precious relics of sepulchral monuments from the Old St.
Peter's, for example the famous Early Christian sarcophagus of Junius Bassus, prefect of Rome, from A.D. 359; the
tomb of Emperor Otto II; and many funeral monuments
of Popes and cardinals, dating from the Renaissance to
modern times.

On high feast days, the great relics of St. Peter's are
exhibited on the balcony above the statue of St. Veronica.
The frieze which runs around the base of the dome bears
the inscription, in blue mosaic letters: *Tu es Petrus et
super hanc petram aedificabo ecclesiam meam et tibi davo
claves regni caelorum*, "Thou art Peter and upon this rock
I will build my church and I will give unto thee the keys
of the kingdom of heaven" (Matthew 16:18, 19). In the
vault of the dome, mosaics by a follower of Raphael:
below, Christ, Mary, and the Apostles; at the center of
the lantern, God the Father.

At the end of the nave is the *tribune*. Above the altar,

45

Bernini's grandiose composition: the soaring throne of St. Peter surrounded by angels and crowned by a halo, in the center of which is the dove, the symbol of the Holy Spirit. The throne encloses the ancient wooden throne inlaid with ivory of the Bishop of Rome. The four great Church Fathers—Ambrose, Athanasius, Augustine, John Chrysostomus—support it with mystic fervor.

To the right of the altar is Bernini's tomb of Urban VIII, with statues personifying Christian Charity and Justice; to the left, Guglielmo della Porta's statue of Pope Paul III, with figures of Wisdom and Justice.

For a survey of the aisles and transepts, we return to the entrance.

Right aisle: The first chapel contains the famous Pietà, an early work of Michelangelo (1499). To its right an ancient spiral column, according to tradition the original column at which Christ was scourged, brought from Jerusalem. It served as model for the columns supporting Bernini's bronze canopy. On the left, under the next arch, the funeral monument of Queen Christina of Sweden, daughter of Gustavus Adolphus, champion of the Reformation. The relief, by Fontana, depicts her conversion to Catholicism at Innsbruck in 1655. At the next pillar to the left is the monument of Margravine Matilda of Tuscany, friend of Pope Gregory VII, who bequeathed her large dominions in central Italy to the Pope in 1115. Bernini's relief represents the German Emperor Henry IV as a penitent at Canossa.

To the right opens the Chapel of the Most Holy Sacrament, resplendent with gold, containing Bernini's gilt-bronze ciborium.

Under the third arch to the right is the tomb of Gregory XIII, the relief referring to his reform of the Julian calendar. Beyond the transept, to the right, Canova's famous tomb of Clement XIII, with two lions, the allegorical figures of Death and Religion, and the Christian virtues of Charity and Hope. At the end, the Chapel of St. Michael, with a copy in mosaic of Guido Reni's painting of St. Michael.

ST. PETER'S. HIGH ALTAR

We pass the tribune to enter the left aisle: Here, in the Cappella Colonna, to the right, the altar of Leo the Great, with a marble relief by Algardi, showing Attila's retreat before the Pope in 452; at the main altar, a picture of the Madonna from the Old St. Peter's.

In the left transept are confessionals for ten languages. In front of the central altar is the tomb of the great composer Palestrina (d. 1594).

Under the next arch, with the tomb of Pius VIII (d. 1830), one enters the *Sacristy* and the *Treasury* containing many precious vestments, monstrances, crucifixes, and papal rings. A visit is recommended.

On the right, we come next to the Chapel of Clement, with the tomb of Gregory the Great, below the altar at the right, and Thorwaldsen's tomb of Pius VII. Further down the aisle, under the arch on the right, the tomb of Leo XI; the relief depicts Henry IV of France abjuring Protestantism. To the left, the tomb of Innocent XI, showing the delivery of Vienna from the Turks by the Polish King Sobieski in 1683.

Further on to the right is the richly gilded Choir

Chapel; beneath the vaulted arch on the left is the tomb of Innocent VIII by the Florentine painter and sculptor Pollaiuolo; to the right, the tomb of Pius X. On the narrow wall of the next chapel is the sepulchral monument of Benedict XV by Canonica.

Under the next arch to the right is the entrance to the *Ascent of the Dome*. An easy spiral ramp takes us first to the terrace above St. Peter's, offering a view of the Square of St. Peter's; from the galleries in the drum is revealed the dizzy height of the dome; the summit affords a magnificent panorama of Rome and the Campagna to the mountains and the sea.

Opposite the entrance to the ramp is Canova's monument to the last Stuarts. Finally, to the right, is the baptismal font—the lid of an ancient porphyry sarcophagus, taken allegedly from the Castel S. Angelo.

We leave St. Peter's and proceed to the colonnade to our left. Here, at the angle where portico and colonnade meet, is the *Portone di Bronzo*, the bronze portal watched over by the Swiss guard, the main entrance to the *Vatican Palace*. Pilgrims ascend by the stairs to the Court of Damasus, built by Bramante under Leo X, or arrive at the end of the entrance hall by the Scala Regia with its grand vista past the statue of Constantine (both the Scala and the statue are works of Bernini) into the interior of the palace.

Visitors proceed onward in the colonnade and pass through the portal at the left into the Via di Porta Angelica; from there, through the Porta Angelica, passing the side entrance of the Vatican Palace, also watched by Swiss Guards, we continue to the left for some ten minutes along the wall of the Vatican, to the official entrance of the papal museums, instituted by Pope Pius XI. We ascend, either by elevator or the spiral stairs, to an anteroom which contains an office of the Vatican postal service. From there to the right through a spacious hallway to a covered loggia, which affords a majestic view of St. Peter's dome and the Vatican gardens. To the right is the Picture Gallery.

DOME OF ST. PETER'S

THE VATICAN PALACE AND THE VATICAN MUSEUMS

Originally the Popes resided not in the Vatican but in the Lateran (p. 65). It was only in 1377, after their return from Avignon, that the Popes established their residence in the then rather exiguous mansion near St. Peter's. Construction of a large new palace was begun by Nicholas V in 1450, and was largely completed in his lifetime. Sixtus IV built the Sistine Chapel (p. 54) between 1473 and 1481, and Innocent VIII the Belvedere (p. 58) between 1486 and 1492; Julius II commissioned Bramante to connect the Belvedere with the main palace by a large court. Bramante is also the architect of the loggias of the Damasus Court. Paul III built the Pauline Chapel, containing Michelangelo's last frescoes (1542-1550). The present appearance of the rooms housing the Collection of Antiquities (p. 56) is due chiefly to Pius VI and Pius VII.

From the loggia we turn to the *Picture Gallery* (Pinacoteca Vaticana), newly built by Pope Pius XI (1922-1932). Brief mention will be made of only the principal works.

Room I: Early works of the Byzantine, Sienese, Umbrian, and Tuscan schools.

Room II: Giotto, the great founder of Florentine painting of the 14th century, and his school. At the center, Giotto's Stefaneschi Altar.

Room III: Early Florentine and Umbrian masters of the 15th century. 245, Filippo Lippi, Madonna and Saints. 247-250, Gentile da Fabriano, Miracles of St. Nicholas of Bari. 251-253, Fra Angelico, Madonna, Angels and Saints; Scenes from the Life of St. Nicholas of Bari. 262, Benozzo Gozzoli, Madonna presenting the girdle to St. Thomas.

Room IV: 270, famous fresco of Melozzo da Forlì, executed in 1477, depicting Sixtus IV's nomination of Bartolo Sacchi as Prefect of the Papal Library. Kneeling before the Pope is Cardinal Giuliano della Rovere, later Pope Julius II; 269, fourteen famous fragments of Melozzo da Forlì's great fresco of the Ascension, from SS. Apostoli (1478-1480).

Room V: On the entrance wall, 275, Lucas Cranach the Elder, Pietà; 290, Giovanni Bellini, Pietà. Room VI: Works of lesser Italian painters.

Room VII: Umbrian school. 317-321, Perugino, Madonna and Saints, Resurrection, and Three Saints.

Room VIII: The famous tapestries from the Sistine Chapel, woven in Brussels in 1515-1516 after cartoons by Raphael: A, Binding of the Sorcerer Elymas; B, The conversion of Paul; C, The stoning of Stephen; D, Peter healing the lame; E, Death of Ananias; F, Peter receiving the Keys; G, The miraculous draught of fishes; H, Paul preaching in Athens; I, The Lystraeans sacrificing before Peter and Paul; L, Paul in prison. Other masterpieces by Raphael are interspersed: 329, Madonna of Foligno (1512); 333, Christ's Transfiguration, Raphael's last work (1517); 334, Coronation of the Virgin (1503).

Room IX: 337, Leonardo da Vinci, St. Jerome; underpainting of the unfinished picture.

Room X: 351, a main work of Titian, Madonna and Saints, (1523). 355, Garofalo, Madonna appearing to Emperor Augustus and the Sybil (1544).

Room XI: 377, Federigo Barocci, Rest on the Flight to Egypt (1573).

Room XII: 384, Domenichino, Communion of St. Jerome (1614); 394, Nicolas Poussin, Martyrdom of St. Erasmus (1630).

Room XIII: 411, Murillo, Mystic Marriage of St. Catherine.

Room XIV: Largely Dutch and Flemish masters.

Room XV: Largely papal portraits. 448, Sir Thomas Lawrence, King George IV of England.

We return to the loggia, and thence left to the entrance to the Collection of Antiquities, the Stanze of Raphael, the Sistine Chapel, and the Borgia Apartments. Bypassing the Collections of Antiquities for the present, we proceed left and then by the stairs to the right to the *Galleria delle Carte Geografiche,* which contains maps of various parts of Italy by Ignazio Danti. The windows afford a view of the Vatican Gardens on the right, and of the Belvedere Court on the left.

At the end of the gallery we enter first, on the left, the room containing modern pictures. Among them is Matejko's colossal painting of the Deliverance of Vienna by King John Sobieski of Poland in 1683. Further along are the *Stanze of Raphael,* the rooms which Raphael decorated in 1508-1520 upon commission of Popes Julius II and Leo X. To inspect the pictures in their chronological order, we pass through the first room, the Stanza dell'Incendio, and pause in the second, the *Stanza della Segnatura,* named for the supreme papal tribunal (Segnatura Apostolica), which convened here in the years 1508-1511.

On the entrance wall is the so-called *Disputà.* What is depicted is not a discussion, but the life and work of the Church in heaven and on earth, the central feature being the Sacrament of the Altar. The lower register shows an assembly of Church Fathers and theologians. To the left

51

is Pope Gregory I enthroned, and at his side St. Jerome with his lion and his translation of the Bible. On the extreme right is Dante, crowned with laurel. In the central register are the patriarchs and prophets of the Old Testament and the apostles and saints of the New. Above are God the Father, Christ, and the Virgin, and below them the dove of the Holy Spirit.

On the opposite wall, as a pendant to Theology, is a representation of Philosophy, in the so-called *School of Athens*. At the center, the great Greek philosophers Plato and Aristotle are shown standing before rich Renaissance buildings. Plato, as the promulgator of the doctrine of ideas, points heavenward; Aristotle, as the realist and founder of the sciences, points earthward. Socrates is in the group at Plato's left, Diogenes lies upon the steps, and in the right foreground is a group of mathematicians and astronomers.

Above the window looking out on the Belvedere Court is the *Parnassus*. Upon the peak of the Greek mountain Apollo is shown surrounded by the nine Muses and the great Greek, Roman, and Italian poets, Homer, Virgil, and Dante. The painting above the opposite window shows the *Promulgation of Civil and Canon Law*. On the left, Emperor Justinian delivers the pandects, or codification of Roman private law, to the jurist Tribonianus; and on the right, Pope Gregory IX presents the decretals to a canon lawyer. The ceiling resumes the principal paintings, showing Theology, Justice, Philosophy, and Poetry.

The small door leads to the *Stanza d'Eliodoro*, painted almost wholly by Raphael 1512-1514. The entrance wall shows *Leo I repelling Attila from Rome*, under the protection of the Apostles Peter and Paul, who hover over him. Opposite is the *Expulsion of Heliodorus*, treasurer of King Seleucus IV of Syria, who attempted to plunder the temple at Jerusalem; according to I Maccabees 3 he was turned back by the miraculous apparition of an angelic horseman. Pope Julius II is borne in from the left. Above the window facing the Belvedere Court is the *Deliverance of St. Peter*. The Apostle is roused from his sleep in prison

STANZE OF RAPHAEL. FIRE IN THE BORGO

and liberated by an angel; on the left, the guards awaken. Opposite is the *Mass of Bolsena*. A Bohemian priest celebrating Mass in Bolsena in 1263 doubted the miraculous transubstantiation of the host into the body of Christ, and was convinced by the sudden appearance of drops of blood in the host. The establishment of the feast of Corpus Christi goes back to this occurrence. Facing the priest is Pope Julius II.

The next room, *Sala di Costantino*, shows among other scenes from the life of Constantine the Great the *Victory of Constantine* over Emperor Maxentius at Ponte Molle (Milvian Bridge) in A.D. 312; this was executed after Raphael's cartoon by his pupil Giulio Romano.

A small door to the left, next to the battle at the Milvian Bridge, leads through the Sala dei Palafrenieri to the *Chapel of Nicholas V*. Its delightful frescoes exhibit scenes from the lives of Sts. Stephen and Lawrence; this is the last work of Fra Angelico da Fiesole, painted 1450-1455.

We return to the first room, the *Stanza dell'Incendio*, painted by Raphael's pupils in 1517 after their master's cartoons. The entrance wall shows the *Fire in the Borgo*

SISTINE CHAPEL

for which the room is named. Fire broke out in the small
papal city (still called Borgo today) in 847, and was extinguished by the sign of the cross made by Pope Leo IV
from the loggia of the Old St. Peter's. On the left is
Virgil's story of Aeneas, who carried his father Anchises
upon his back from the burning ruins of Troy; Aeneas is
accompanied by his wife Creusa and his small son As-
canius. The opposite wall shows *Leo IV's Victory over the
Saracens* at Ostia in 849. The Pope's features are those
of Leo X. The wall with the window shows *Leo III's Oath*
before Charlemagne on Christmas Eve of 800, with similar contemporary allusions in the portraiture.

We return through the gallery of modern paintings and
proceed through the small corridor at the left to the
Sistine Chapel. The chapel is named for Sixtus IV, who
built it in 1473-1481. It is the papal chapel proper, and
serves for papal elections and for particular, solemn serv-
ices of the Pope. Sixtus IV had the longitudinal walls
decorated by the most famous Florentine and Umbrian
painters. We name below the outstanding paintings. Pictures from the life of Moses cover the left wall, looking

from the altar, and parallel scenes from the life of Christ
the right.

Left: 1, Pinturicchio, Moses and his wife on their jour-
ney to Egypt; Circumcision of his son. 2, Botticelli, The
Burning Bush; Moses slaying the Egyptians; Moses driv-
ing the shepherds from the well. 5, Botticelli, Destruction
of Korah's company. 6, Signorelli and Bartolo della Gatta,
Moses and the Tables of the Law; Investiture of Joshua;
Mourning for Moses.

Right: 1, Perugino and Pinturicchio, Baptism of Christ.
2, Botticelli, Christ heals the leper; The temptation of
Christ. 3, Ghirlandajo, Vocation of Peter and Andrew. 5,
Perugino, The transmission of the keys.

Pope Julius II commissioned Michelangelo to decorate
the ceiling in 1508-1512. Paul III ordered the fresco on
the altar wall, executed in 1534-1541. The Sistine Chapel
thus became an incomparable artistic whole, displaying
fully Michelangelo's power and the wealth of his artistic
imagination. In the architectonic sectioning of the vaulting
we see the *Prophets* and *Sibyls*. To the left of the altar:
1, Jeremiah reflecting; 2, The Persian Sibyl reading;
3, Ezekiel with the scroll; 4, The Erythraean Sibyl with
a book; 5, Joel reading the scroll; 6 (over the door),
Zacharias turning the pages of a book; 7, The Delphic
Sibyl with a scroll; 8, Isaiah leaning on a book; 9, The
Cumaean Sibyl opening a book; 10, Daniel writing; 11,
the Libyan Sibyl grasping a book; 12, Jonah escaping
from the maw of the whale.

In the central paintings of the ceiling, Michelangelo
proceeded from figures on a smaller scale, near the entrance, to ones of increasing size: 1, God separates light
from darkness; 2, He creates sun, moon, and vegetation;
3, He creates the fish of the sea and the fowl of the air;
4, From His index finger life streams into the body of
newly fashioned Adam; 5, Creation of Eve; 6, The fall of
man and the expulsion from Paradise; 7, Noah's thank-
offering; 8, The Deluge; 9, Noah's drunkenness.

On the altar wall is the gigantic *Last Judgment*. Above,
in the center, Christ as Judge with the Mother of God,

surrounded by apostles and saints. St. Bartholomew is shown carrying his flayed skin. Angels bear the instruments of the Passion—cross, nails, and chains. At the left, the blessed soar upwards; at the right, the damned are drawn and thrust downwards. On the earth the dead arise, amidst the trumpeting of angels. On the right, following Dante's description, is the underworld with the boatman Charon; above is Minos, judge of the dead.

We return to the Stanze of Raphael. From the Sala dell'Incendio we pass through the door at the left and down the stairs into the *Appartamento Borgia,* where Pope Alexander VI (Rodrigo Borgia) and his family lived. The rich furnishing and the frescoes of Pinturicchio are particularly worth noticing. Room II: Scenes from the life of Christ, The descent of the Holy Ghost, The Assumption. Room III: On the entrance wall, the story of St. Susanna is on the left, that of St. Barbara on the right. The rear wall has a Disputation of St. Catherine of Alexandria (whose features are those of Lucrezia Borgia) with Emperor Maximian. Far to the right is the Turkish prince and poet, Djem, who opposed his brother, Sultan Bajazet II, and resided at the papal court as captive. On the exit wall, to the left, are the holy hermits Paul and Anthony in the desert, and on the right the Visitation. On the window wall is the Martyrdom of St. Sebastian. Room IV: Allegories of the seven liberal arts—Grammar, Dialectic, Rhetoric, Geometry, Arithmetic, Music, Astrology.

We return to the *Collections of Antiquities.* (For introductory remarks see p. 127 ff.).

I, *Sala a Croce Greca* (in the form of a Greek cross): At its center, on the floor, ancient mosaics; adjacent, the porphyry sarcophagus of Constantia (died 354), the daughter of Emperor Constantine the Great. Cupids are shown at the vintage, amidst rich foliage (No. 566). Opposite (No. 589) the porphyry sarcophagus of St. Helena, mother of Constantine the Great, showing the victory of mounted Romans over Persians and Germans.

II, *Sala Rotonda* (a domed structure modeled on the Pantheon): On the floor is a large mosaic with sea-divinities. Magnificent fountain basin of porphyry. We proceed from left to right: 550, colossal statue of Emperor Claudius as Jupiter; 547, Sea-god, with a vine garland and dolphins in his beard, perhaps a personification of the Bay of Baiae near Naples; 542 and 546, colossal statues of goddesses, copies of works of the school of Phidias; 544, colossal bronze statue of Hercules; 545, colossal bust of Antinoüs, favorite of Emperor Hadrian, who is also shown in the colossal statue, 540; 539, famous colossal head of the Zeus of Otricoli.

III, *Sala delle Muse* (named for a related group of statues of the Muses, here assembled, 499, 503, 505, 508); 525, on the left, is a herma of the great Athenian statesman Pericles; 519, on the right, the great philosopher Plato; 514, his teacher Socrates; 521, the tragic poet Euripides.

IV, *Sala degli Animali:* This room has numerous much restored representations of animals.

V, *Galleria delle Statue:* No. 250 in the row at the right is the famous Eros of Centocelle, a Roman copy of a work of the first quarter of the 4th century B.C., showing the god of love looking yearningly at his victim. 253, a sea-god with a tense, melancholy expression, is of the Pergamene school (3rd century B.C.). 264, a youthful Apollo watching a lizard on a tree trunk; this is a copy of an original of Praxiteles of the 4th century B.C. From here to

VI, *Galleria dei Busti:* This room has numerous portraits of Roman emperors. 292, to the right, above, is Caracalla. 273, below, the youthful Octavius, later Emperor Augustus. Near the entrance, to the left, 388, funeral monument from the end of the Republic, portraying a husband and wife with dignified simplicity.

We return to the Galleria delle Statue. Here, along the window wall, to 406, a Resting Satyr, modeled upon a famous work of the 4th century. To the right of the entrance into Room VIII, 407, a magnificent votive relief, a Greek original of the mid-5th century B.C.—Youth attended by a slave with strigil and oil flask.

VIII, *Gabinetto delle Maschere:* The floor has a mosaic

with theater masks, hence the name of the room. 474 is a Roman copy of Praxiteles' Aphrodite of Cnidos of the mid-4th century B.C.

Back to the Galleria delle Statue. Here, against the short wall, the Sleeping Ariadne (414), a Hellenistic work of the beginning of the 2nd century B.C.

Returning through the Sala degli Animali, we find, on the left,

IX, *Cortile del Belvedere:* The first corner alcove on the right contains the famous group of Laocoon and his two sons strangled by the serpents sent by Apollo (74); this is a Rhodian work of the second half of the 1st century B.C. To the left in the second corner alcove, the Apollo Belvedere (92), after a Greek original of the mid-4th century B.C. As a personification of nobility and purity the god wards off the vulgarity of the world with his bow. On the walls, two original fragments of a metope, and of the frieze of the Parthenon of Athens (*c.* 440 B.C.). Further to the left, past the Perseus by Canova of 1800 (32), to the alcove with the so-called Antinoüs Belvedere, actually an attractively benignant figure of Hermes, after an original of the mid-4th century B.C. (53).

We return to the fountain court, and opposite the entrance pass into the circular Room X, with a view of the Castel S. Angelo, Monte Mario, and, on the right, the Pincio and the Villa Medici. In the room at the left is the famous Apoxyomenus (scraper), an athlete scraping dust and oil from his body after the exertions of the palaestra; this is a copy of a work of Lysippus of the last quarter of the 4th century B.C. At the wall on the left is the sarcophagus of L. Cornelius Scipio, member of the famous Roman family, who conquered Corsica in 259 B.C. In the room at the right is the Torso Belvedere, which was so much admired by Michelangelo; it is an original of the latter half of the 1st century B.C. by the Greek artist Apollonius.

On the right is the entrance to the Egyptian Museum, on the left a staircase leads to the Etruscan Museum and the Collection of Vases (see below).

Braccio Nuovo: At the right longitudinal wall No. 11,

VATICAN MUSEUMS. SALA ROTONDA

a Wise Silenus with the infant Dionysus on his arm (end of the 4th century B.C.). No. 14, famous statue of Emperor Augustus, from the villa of his wife Livia, at Primaporta. The relief on the corselet shows the consecration to Mars of the recovered Parthian standards (p. 25), with divinities and symbolic figures of the subjugated provinces of Germania and Dacia. No. 26 is a portrait of Emperor Titus. Past the rectangular niche a portrait of Emperor Trajan (41). Resuming along the left longitudinal wall, we find 64, a statue of the great Athenian orator Demosthenes, after an original of 280 B.C. All the passion of his patriotism is concentrated in his posture (the hands are missing). At the center of the niche the Nile (106) appears as the god of Egypt's fertility. The sixteen children climbing to the cornucopia represent the sixteen cubits of the beneficent flood of the river. No. 123 is the Doryphorus or spear-bearer, a copy of a famous bronze by Polyclitus of Argos, of the mid-5th century B.C. The statue typifies youthful virility and beauty in rhythmic motion. No. 126 is a statue of Emperor Domitian in armor; the nymph and bull, triton and dolphin on the corselet represent land and sea.

The exit from the Braccio Nuovo leads to the exhibition room of the library (p. 62), or we may retrace our steps through the rooms to the entrance stairway. At its head and to the left are the Etruscan Museum and the *Collection of Vases,* Greek, South Italian, and Etruscan. Of these, only a few famous specimens will be mentioned.

Room V: Isolated in the center an amphora of the Athenian vase-painter Exekias (*c.* 550 B.C.); black figures with incised inner details against a red background. The front shows the Homeric heroes Achilles and Ajax at a board game; the rear, the immortal twins Castor and Pollux and their mother Leda. Case D: 25, a drinking cup of yellow clay from Sparta, shows Atlas bearing the vault of heaven and an eagle tearing at Prometheus' liver (*c.* 550 B.C.). Case E: Prize amphorae which were presented, filled with oil, at the athletic contests in Athens (6th century B.C.).

Room VI: At the center, a mixing-bowl for water and wine; colored designs on a white ground: Hermes brings the new-born Dionysus to the nymphs (mid-5th century B.C.). Case I: Numerous drinking bowls in red-figured technique. The outline of the figures is drawn on the red ground of the vase, and the surrounding space is then filled out with a black varnish. This technique, which flourished from about 530 B.C. onwards, permitted greater freedom in composition and expressiveness of figures. Case K: No. 3 shows the child Hermes stealing the cattle of Apollo; from the workshop of Brygos, an Athenian painter of the early 5th century B.C. Below, No. 26, a hydria or water jug of about 470 B.C., showing Apollo riding over the sea on a winged tripod. In the semicircular corridor VII, No. 6 in Case M shows Jason, the hero of the Argo, spewed forth by a sea monster while his patroness Athene looks on; approximate date, 480 B.C. No. 10, an oenochoe, or wine jug, of about 440 B.C., shows Menelaus encountering his faithless Helen after the sack of Troy; Aphrodite revives his love, and he lets his sword drop.

VATICAN LIBRARY

Room VIII: Etruscan and South Italian ware. The terra-cotta group shows the dying Adonis (2nd century B.C.).

We retrace our steps through these rooms and enter the *Etruscan Museum*. For remarks on the Etruscans see p. 2.

Room I: Etruscan sarcophagi. No. 27, at the left of the entrance, shows the destruction of the children of Niobe (5th century B.C.). At the right of the entrance to Room II is a distinguished official riding in a carriage and accompanied by lictors (3rd century B.C.). No. 59 on the left: Sarcophagus of a warrior, with a nuptial procession (5th century B.C.).

Room II: This room exhibits the contents of the Regolini-Galassi tomb (named for its discoverers), found at Cerveteri in 1836. A princely tomb, it contained rich weapons, a chariot, gold ornaments, bronze vessels, tripods, and the like (7th century B.C.).

Room III: Large collection of bronzes, fragments of big Etruscan and Roman bronze figures, among them magnificent specimens, engraved bronze Etruscan mirrors, gold ornaments, ivory work, etc.

Room IV: Decorative reliefs in clay, cinerary urns of terra cotta or alabaster, portraits.

We return to the exit at the staircase. Opposite, we find the *Sala della Biga:* This room is named after the chariot exhibited there, which dates from the middle of the 1st century A.D.; the horses are modern. On the right, No. 608, a stately statue, over life-size, of a deity akin to Dionysus, after an original of the 4th century B.C. No. 612 is a togaed portrait of a Roman noble of the Empire. No. 618, a discus-thrower, is a copy of the Greek sculptor Myron's famous masterpiece of about 450 B.C.; the head is modern.

We return to descend the stairs, and proceed straight ahead to the *Museo Profano della Biblioteca.* Room I: The niche at the right of the entrance holds a bronze portrait of Augustus, that to the left a bronze portrait of Nero.

We follow the long gallery to the second entrance on the left, which leads to the *Exhibition Room* of the library. In the cases, many valuable manuscripts, incunabula, and authographs. Particularly notable are a Greek New Testament, and a Virgil of the 5th century A.D., Botticelli's illustrations for Dante's *Divine Comedy,* and autographs of Thomas Aquinas, Martin Luther, Michelangelo, and Henry VIII of England.

We return to the gallery and continue to the *Museo Sacro della Biblioteca,* which has finds from the catacombs and a collection of Greek papyri.

The door following, to the right, leads to the *Sala delle Nozze Aldobrandini,* which has a series of famous antique frescoes. The best known is the Aldobrandini Nuptials, at the center of the right wall. The Greek god Dionysus waits at the nuptial couch, on which Aphrodite is counseling his bride. This is a Roman copy of the Augustan period, after a Greek work of the 4th century B.C. In addition there are the Odyssey landscapes, showing Odysseus among the Lastrygonians; with the sorceress Circe; at the entrance to Hades. These date from the 1st century B.C.

FAMOUS CHURCHES

INTRODUCTION

MODERN Romans maintain that their city possesses so many churches and larger chapels that a man may worship in a different one every day of the year. The following notes can glance at only the most important.

The first great age of church building in Rome was that of the Early Christian basilicas and sepulchral churches which began with the mighty constructions of Emperor Constantine. These include the Old St. Peter's (p. 42), S. Giovanni in Laterano (p. 65), S. Agnese fuori le Mura (p. 99), and S. Costanza (p. 99). The pillared basilica, with its nave raised to a clerestory, narrower aisles, apse at the lengthening of the nave, rich decoration in figured mosaic, survived in the following centuries also, and may be seen in S. Maria Maggiore (p. 77) or S. Paolo fuori le Mura (p. 90), where, despite modern restorations, the ancient impression can be experienced at its purest, unspoiled by Baroque additions.

Romanesque art, which created the great cathedrals of France and Germany, is not represented in any considerable Roman building; and Gothic only by the Dominican Church, S. Maria sopra Minerva (p. 74). In church architecture also, Rome's rebirth begins with the Renaissance. To this period belong S. Maria del Popolo (p. 105) and S. Maria della Pace (p. 79). But it was in the High Renaissance that Rome assumed leadership in newer church architecture: with Bramante, who planned the ideal structure of S. Pietro in Montorio (p. 82) and the court of S. Maria della Pace (p. 79), and Michelangelo, who designed St. Peter's. The High Renaissance developed the vaulted structure, created new proportions in large spaces, and articulated them with Doric, Ionic, and Corinthian orders,

S. GIOVANNI IN LATERANO

borrowed from ancient buildings like the Colosseum. Later
the Jesuit Church of Gesù, by Vignola (p. 74), became the
most influential model for the church architecture of all
of Europe.

From the accentuation of the media employed by the
High Renaissance, the Baroque style in church and palace
architecture developed. It is to this, primarily, that modern
Rome owes its homogeneous appearance. Baroque churches
are distinguished by the picturesque elaboration of façades,
multiplication of columns, vivid contrasts of light and
shadow, sweeping lines everywhere in motion, restless
effects in the exteriors, floor plans of the utmost boldness
in the interiors, numerous oval spaces, domes with dra-
matic lighting, close interrelation of sculpture and painting
with architecture. They are creations of the most amazing
genius ever shown by architects. The masters of Baroque
in Rome are Lorenzo Bernini, in S. Andrea al Quirinale
(p. 73), and Francesco Borromini in S. Carlo alle Quattro
Fontane (p. 73) and S. Agnese (p. 78).

64

We begin with the *Church of S. Giovanni in Laterano*, on the Piazza di S. Giovanni in Laterano. The obelisk of rose-colored granite in the center of the square is the tallest in Rome—105 ft. high. Originally brought from Thebes in Upper Egypt, and placed in the Circus Maximus, it is inscribed with the name of Thutmose IV (15th century B.C.).

BAPTISTERY OF S. GIOVANNI

The Lateran is the oldest of the Roman basilicas. It derives its name from the palace of the ancient Roman noble family of the Laterani, which Emperor Constantine presented to the Pope and in which he built the first Lateran Church. The old church was a pillared basilica of five aisles, with a broad transept before the apse. Only its general outline is retained in the present structure.

The main entrance is on the Piazza di Porta S. Giovanni; the handsome Baroque façade is by Alessandro Galilei (1735). The vivid colossal statues, about 20 ft. high, on the balustrade, are visible at a great distance. The interior was transformed by Francesco Borromini, about

65

1650. The niches of the piers contain twelve colossal statues of the apostles (School of Bernini). At the center of the transept, over the high altar, is a Gothic tabernacle which enshrines precious relics.

The frescoes in the right transept, dating from 1603, present events in the life of Emperor Constantine the Great. On the right, the foundation and consecration of the Lateran basilica. On the left, the baptism of Constantine, and the envoys of the Emperor greeting Pope Sylvester at Mount Soracte, near Rome. At the right of the choir is the monument to Pope Innocent III, erected by Leo XIII.

In the apse are modern copies of the mosaics of 1290: the Cross, and the dove of the Holy Ghost on the hill of the heavenly Jerusalem, from which four rivers flow down to water deer and lambs. On the left are Mary and the kneeling donor, Pope Nicholas IV, with Sts. Peter and Paul. On the right, Sts. John and Andrew. Nearby, on a smaller scale, the saints of the Franciscan order, Francis of Assisi and Anthony of Padua. Beneath are the river Jordan, the Apostles, and the artists who executed the work, Jacopo Torriti on the left, and Friar Jacopo da Camerino on the right.

In the transept, to the left of the choir, the tomb of Leo XIII. Frescoes above, to the right: The miracle of the appearance of an image of Christ on the wall of the Lateran basilica, and the foundation by Constantine; to the left: Sts. Peter and Paul appear to the ailing Constantine in a dream and promise him recovery through baptism. Next is the triumph of Constantine.

On the back of the first pillar of the nave, a fresco by Giotto, showing Boniface VIII proclaiming the jubilee of 1300.

The last chapel of the left aisle gives access to a handsome cloister of the 13th century.

We leave the church by the exit at the right end of the transept, and find, immediately to the left, the old *Baptistery*, the oldest baptismal church in Rome; the legend that Constantine the Great received baptism here is, however,

S. CLEMENTE. INTERIOR

without foundation. The circular building is of the 5th century A.D.; an ancient bath of green basalt serves as font. The bronze doors of the Oratory of John the Baptist at the right of the entrance are antique. Opposite the entrance is the Porticus of St. Venantius, originally the vestibule of the baptismal chapel. In the apse, at the left, fine mosaics of the 5th century, with charming gold arabesques on a blue ground. Adjacent the Chapel of St. Venantius, with mosaics of the 7th century: the symbols of the evangelists, the cities of Bethlehem and Jerusalem, the eight martyrs of Salona, Christ between angels, Madonna between saints. The fourth door at the left of the entrance leads to the Chapel of St. John the Evangelist, with mosaics of the 5th century: birds and flowers on a gold ground.

To the left of the Baptistery, the Via di S. Giovanni takes us, in five minutes, to a small square with the *Church of S. Clemente*. Dedicated to St. Clement, the third successor of St. Peter, this is one of the oldest basilicas in

Rome. Through the atrium we enter first the upper church of 1108, which consists of three aisles, separated by two rows of antique columns. The choir screens and ambos, of the 6th century, belonged to the lower church. On the triumphal arch, at the center, mosaics of the 12th century: bust of Christ with the symbols of the evangelists; below, saints; Bethlehem on the left and Jerusalem on the right. On the vaulting, Christ on the Cross, with John and Mary, framed in rich foliage; below, thirteen lambs. At the beginning of the left aisle, the Chapel of St. Catherine of Alexandria, with famous frescoes by Masolino (c. 1431). Above, left: St. Catherine refuses to worship a pagan idol; in captivity she teaches the daughters of the king. Below, she is shown in disputation with scholars before Emperor Maximian.

Descent to the lower church is through the sacristy in the right aisle. This was built after the 4th century, and was much larger and more magnificent than the later upper church. Subsequently it was covered over, and excavated only in the 19th century. In the vestibule are three frescoes of the 11th and 12th centuries. On the right wall, the miracle of St. Clement: One day in the year the waters of the Black Sea retire, and the grave of St. Clement, on the floor of the sea, can be visited. There a mother finds sleeping a child that had been drowned, and awakens him to life. Further to the right: The relics of St. Cyril, apostle to the Slavs, are removed to S. Clemente from the Vatican. The saint is buried in the church. The left aisle has frescoes of the 9th century, illustrating stories of the Old and New Testaments. In the nave, at the left, scenes from the life of St. Clement (9th century). Farther to the left, three pictures from the life of St. Alexius.

At the end of the left aisle, or directly from the apse of the upper church, access to the sanctuary of Mithras under the lower church. Mithras was the Persian deity whose religion was spread over the entire Roman Empire. A relief shows Mithras slaying the bull.

Adjacent to S. Clemente the Via Labicana, which we follow, to the right, to Via Merulana, then along the Via

S. PIETRO IN VINCOLI

Merulana to Via Giovanni Lanza on the left, then Via Giovanni Lanza until it joins Via Cavour. Here a steep staircase ascends to a palace with a loggia and three bays. These are the remains of the palace of the Borgia family—Pope Alexander VI, his ambitious son Cesare, and his beautiful daughter Lucrezia.

We pass under the arch to the Piazza S. Pietro in Vincoli, and, to the left, to the *Church of S. Pietro in Vincoli.* This was founded by Empress Eudoxia, wife of the Western Emperor Valentinian III. Eudoxia presented the church with the chains of St. Peter, which were miraculously joined, according to legend, with a portion preserved in Constantinople.

The porch, a work of the early Renaissance, was built about 1475. The interior is a three-aisled basilica with twenty antique Doric columns. In the nave, at the pillar to the left of the entrance, is the tomb of the Pollaiuolo brothers, the great sculptors of the early Renaissance. Above, a votive offering to avert the plague of 1476. At the side of the first altar of the left aisle is the Renaissance

tomb of the great German philosopher and Cardinal, Niko-
laus Krebs, called Cusanus (1464); St. Peter is shown
between the Cardinal and an angel. Under the high altar
is the handsome bronze Renaissance tabernacle containing
the chains of St. Peter.

S. PRASSEDE. MOSAIC APSE

At the end of the right aisle are the remains of
Michelangelo's design for a monumental, many-figured
tomb of Julius II (died 1513), planned originally for St.
Peter's, but never completed. At the center, the figure of
Moses, filled with holy wrath. Also by Michelangelo are
the statues of Rachel, on the left, and Leah, on the right,
symbolizing respectively the active and the contemplative
life. Other figures belonging to the tomb are in Florence
and Paris. The remaining figures were executed by pupils
of the master.

We retrace our steps along the Via Giovanni Lanza, up
to the Medieval fortress tower, then left, along Via S.
Martino ai Monti, and before this ends, left through the
Via S. Prassede to the *Church of S. Prassede.*

S. MARIA MAGGIORE

The three-aisled church has sixteen granite columns. The mosaics, of the 9th century, are very impressive: On the triumphal arch, Christ with angels in the new Jerusalem; on the arch of the apse, the Lamb of the Apocalypse with the seven candelabra, the symbols of the evangelists, and the twenty-four elders; in the dome of the apse, the Redeemer and saints; underneath, Peter and Paul, and Pope Paschal I. The Pope is distinguished by a square halo, as he is shown during his lifetime, in the act of consecrating the church. At the feet of Christ is the river Jordan; underneath, Christ surrounded by lambs. Third in the right aisle, the chapel of St. Zeno; over the ancient beams at its entrance, additional mosaics of the 9th century: Madonna and saints, Christ and the apostles. In the vaulting, four angels support the circle surrounding the head of Christ.

The Via S. Prassede leads to the square before *S. Maria Maggiore*, with its column from the Basilica of Constantine (p. 32). Pious legend relates that on the night of August 5, 352, the Virgin appeared in a dream to Pope Liberius and the Roman patrician John, and bade them build her a church on the spot which they would find covered with snow on the following day; thus the Basilica Liberiana was built here. It received Christ's manger as its most precious relic; and as the eldest and most important of the many churches dedicated to the Virgin in Rome, it is called S. Maria Maggiore, St. Mary Major.

The façade dates from the 18th century. In the loggia, handsome mosaics from the earlier façade, of about 1300: In the upper center, Christ enthroned and surrounded by angels; below, on the left, the dream of Pope Liberius and the patrician John; on the right, the two meet and sketch the plan of the church in the snow.

The interior is a three-aisled basilica. The nave, with its forty Ionic columns and mosaic frieze, belongs to the structure of Sixtus III. The pictures on the triumphal arch and the longitudinal frieze are the most important monuments of late Roman painting preserved to us. At the crown of the arch is the Apocalyptic throne, with diadem, purple, and triumphal cross. At the sides are, to the left, Paul, and to the right, Peter. Below, on the left, are the Annunciation to Mary and Joseph, the Adoration of the Magi, the Slaughter of the Innocents. Corresponding on the right: The Presentation at the Temple and the instruction for the Flight to Egypt, the encounter of the Holy Family with the King of Egypt, the Magi before Herod. Quite at the bottom, Jerusalem on the left and Nazareth on the right. The mosaics of the left frieze illustrate stories of the patriarchs Abraham, Isaac, and Jacob in twenty-one pictures; those on the right, events in the lives of Moses and Joshua.

Before the high altar, with four columns of porphyry and an ancient porphyry bath containing the body of the Apostle Matthew, is the confessio, with its relic of the manger. In front the marble statue of Pope Pius IX.

The apse of the tribune contains mosaics of 1295: the Coronation of Mary, with Sts. Peter and Paul, other saints, and nine choirs of angels; the small kneeling figure is Pope Nicholas IV.

In the right transept, the Chapel of Sixtus V, resplendent with gold. His tomb, at the left, has his statue and reliefs showing events of his office. At the left, the tomb of Pius V. Opposite this chapel, in the left transept, is the Borghese Chapel, erected by Paul V (Borghese) in 1611; his tomb is against the left wall; on the right, the tomb of Clement VIII (Ippolito Aldobrandini). Over the altar is one of the numerous pictures of the Madonna traditionally ascribed to St. Luke.

We leave the church by its rear exit, and find ourselves on the Piazza dell'Esquilino, upon which rises an obelisk from the Mausoleum of Augustus. We follow straight ahead the Via Agostino Depreti and its continuation as Via Quattro Fontane until we come to the crossing which is decorated by four fountains. At the left corner is the small *Church of S. Carlo alle Quattro Fontane,* an outstanding example of Borromini's Baroque architecture, built in 1640-1667. The interior exhibits bold ingenuity in a very limited space.

Proceeding left from the church on the Via del Quirinale, we arrive after a few minutes at *S. Andrea al*

Quirinale, to the left, opposite the Quirinal Palace. Built by Bernini in 1678 for the nephew of Innocent X, it is another great example of Roman Baroque.

CHURCHES AT THE CENTER OF THE CITY

Behind the Palazzo Venezia, at the corner of the Via del Plebiscito and the Piazza Gesù, is the *Church of Gesù,* which has exerted the profoundest influence on the development of church architecture throughout Europe after the High Renaissance. It was built by Vignola and Giacomo della Porta in 1568-1575 as the principal church of the Jesuits. The façade bears statues of saints of the order. In the interior the nave, become dominant, diminishes the aisles which are now reduced to side chapels. The ceiling painting, by Baciccio, glorifies the name of Jesus. In the left transept is the rich altar and the reliquary of St. Ignatius Loyola, the founder of the Jesuit order. The marble group at the right represents the victory of Christianity over heretics; that on the left represents the Faith with chalice and host, being worshiped by a heathen king. Opposite is the altar of St. Francis Xavier, the missionary to the Indies.

Opposite the Piazza del Gesù, the Via del Gesù leads to the Piazza della Minerva. Here, an obelisk borne by an elephant, which comes from the temple of the Egyptian goddess Isis; the temple is still underground in the near vicinity. The elephant is a work of Bernini (1667).

The *Church of S Maria sopra Minerva* is erected on the ruins of a temple of Minerva built by Emperor Domitian, whence its name. It is the principal church of the Dominicans, as the Gesù is that of the Jesuits. The adjoining monastery was the seat of the Inquisition; it was here that Galileo, the founder of modern physics, was condemned in 1633.

With its three lofty vaulted aisles, this is the only purely Gothic church in Rome. It was built about 1280, and newly painted in the 19th century. It is filled with historical monuments and works of art, of which only the most im-

74

CHURCH OF GESU

portant are mentioned here. Right aisle: In the fourth
chapel a beautiful Annunciation on gold ground, by Antoniazzo Romano (works, 1461-1508). In the foreground,
Cardinal Torquemada commends three poor girls to the
Virgin; this commemorates the fraternity established in
1460 for providing dowries for needy girls. In the right
transept, immediately to the right, is the Caraffa Chapel
with frescoes by the Florentine Filippino Lippi (1489).
On the right the great doctor of the Church, Thomas
Aquinas, defending Catholic doctrine against the heretics.
Over the altar, an Annunciation, with the donor, Cardinal
Caraffa. On the wall at the back is the Assumption. At

the left, the tomb of Pope Paul IV. In the choir, the tombs of the two Medici Popes, on the left Leo X, on the right Clement VII. The high altar enshrines the body of St. Catherine of Siena, who was instrumental in effecting the return of the Pope from Avignon to Rome (p. 8). At the left of the high altar, the Risen Christ with the Cross, a masterpiece of Michelangelo (1514) in which Christian mysticism has been combined with the beauty of the nude body of ancient art. In the left transept, the Chapel of St. Dominic, with the tomb of Pope Benedict XIII. In the sacristy at the right, the death chamber of St. Catherine of Siena is shown.

We leave the church by the chapel left of the choir. Here, under an ever-burning light, is the tombstone of the great Florentine painter Fra Angelico da Fiesole, who died in the adjoining monastery in 1455.

The Via di S. Ignazio leads to the delightful Piazza di S. Ignazio, built in the most elaborate Rococo style by Raguzzini for Pope Benedict XIII. At the left is the mighty façade of the *Church of S. Ignazio* by Algardi. Dedicated to the founder of the Jesuit order, S. Ignazio is the other great Jesuit church in Rome (Gesù being one). The interior is dominated by the magnificent ceiling fresco of the Jesuit Father Pozzo, the master of perspective. This shows St. Ignatius entering paradise. The fresco is borne by allegorical figures of the four continents. The best view of this is had by standing on the round marble slab in the center of the nave.

From the Piazza di S. Ignazio, the Via del Seminario leads to the Piazza della Rotonda, with its fountain surmounted by an obelisk. Like that before S. Maria sopra Minerva it comes from the temple of Isis. Here is the impressive façade of the *Pantheon*. In 609 Emperor Phocas presented the building to Pope Boniface IV, who dedicated it to the Virgin. It became *S. Maria della Rotonda* and thus the marvelous structure survived the ruin of centuries.

Along with the so-called Tempio della Fortuna Virilis (p. 122) the Pantheon is the only completely preserved

PANTHEON

classical temple in Rome. The architrave of the portico, with its sixteen granite columns 41 ft. high, mentions the name of Agrippa, the general, and son-in-law of Augustus. Agrippa built the first Pantheon, together with large baths, in 27 B.C. But that structure was damaged by lightning; the present Pantheon is a completely new edifice erected by Emperor Hadrian in the 2nd century A.D. The gilt-bronze tiles of the roof were removed to Constantinople in 662. The bronze beams supporting the roof of the portico were used by Pope Urban VIII in 1632 for the columns of the high altar in St. Peter's and for cannon for the Castel S. Angelo. The bronze doors are ancient. The interior is illuminated only by the aperture in the center of the dome, 29 ft. in diameter. The diameter of the perfectly circular interior—142 ft.—equals the height of the dome; the interior is the most harmoniously proportioned in the world.

Leaving the Pantheon, the narrow Salita dei Crescenzi on the left leads to the Palazzo Madama. It takes its name from Madama Margareta of Austria, natural daughter of Emperor Charles V, married first to a Medici, and then, unhappily, to a Farnese. The palace is now the seat of the Italian Senate.

Opposite is the *Church of S. Luigi de' Francesi,* the national church of the French, dedicated in 1589 to St. Louis IX of France. In the second chapel at the right of the three-aisled interior are famous frescoes from the life of St. Cecilia by Domenichino. In the left aisle: At the right of the first column, a monument to the great landscape painter Claude Lorrain (1836). On the walls of the fifth chapel, Caravaggio's famous Scenes from the life of St. Matthew.

The second small street at the left of the church leads, again to the left, to the Piazza S. Agostino. Here, to the right, stairs ascend to the *Church of S. Agostino.* It was the first domed church in Rome, built with blocks from the Colosseum in 1479-1483. On the wall next to the entrance to the three-aisled interior is the much revered marble Madonna del Parto—Our Lady of Easy Birth—by Jacopo Sansovino (1521). On the high altar, a painting of the Madonna, traditionally attributed to St. Luke, and said to have been brought from Constantinople.

From S. Luigi de' Francesi a small street at the left, and an aperture lead to the Piazza Navona. Dominating the piazza is the handsome *Church of S. Agnese,* built by Borromini and Rainaldi in 1625-1650. The interior, by Rainaldi, is in the form of a Greek cross. Over the door is the tomb of Pope Innocent X. At the altar of the left transept is an ancient statue transformed to represent St. Sebastian. A stair leads down to the subterranean vaults of the Circus of Domitian, where, according to tradition, St. Agnes suffered martyrdom.

A short street at the right of the church leads to the Via dell'Anima. We turn to the right. At the end of the street, to the left, is the *Church of S. Maria dell'Anima,* the national church of the old German Empire, to which the

Netherlands also belonged. Inside, many German and Dutch tombs. The ceiling frescoes and the stained-glass window over the main entrance are by Ludwig Seitz. Giulio Romano's painting of the Holy Family on the high altar is a donation of Jakob Fugger, the rich banker of Augsburg. In the choir to the right, the tomb of Pope Adrian VI, the last German Pope, teacher of Emperor Charles V; statues on the tomb represent Justice, Wisdom, Fortitude, and Moderation. On the left, the tomb of Duke Karl-Friedrich of Cleve-Juelich-Berg, who died on a pilgrimage to Rome in the jubilee of 1575.

Facing the church we turn to the right and walk around it to reach, through the Vicolo della Pace, the *Church of S. Maria della Pace*, built in 1484, and later provided with a semicircular portico. Inside the domed octagonal structure, above the first chapel to the right, the famous Four Sibyls of Raphael. The fresco over the altar of the chapel—Madonna between Sts. Bridget and Catherine, with the donor, Cardinal Ponzetti, kneeling—is by Baldassare Peruzzi (1516). Through the sacristy or by the Vicolo dell'Arco della Pace 5, outside the church, one enters the fine cloister built by Bramante.

From the square in front of the church the narrow streets Via del Teatro Pace and its continuation, Vicolo della Cancelleria, take us back to the Corso Vittorio Emanuele. At its center, on the right, is the rich façade of the *Church of S. Andrea della Valle*, executed in 1665. The interior is a Latin cross, with a large dome, completed by Maderna in 1650. Far into the nave, on the left, is the tomb of Pope Pius II (Enea Silvio Piccolomini), on the right that of Pius III Piccolomini (1503). In the dome, the Glory of Paradise by Lanfranco, and in the spandrils the famous Four Evangelists by Domenichino (1623). His too are the frescoes in the apse: John the Baptist directing Sts. Andrew and John to Christ; Christ summoning Sts. Peter and Andrew; Scourging of St. Andrew; St. Andrew sees the cross of his martyrdom. Beneath are Christian Virtues.

THE TIBER ISLAND (ISOLA TIBERINA) AND TRASTEVERE

Behind the Theater of Marcellus (p. 122) the *Ponte Fabricio,* with four-headed hermae on its balustrade, leads to the Tiber Island. The bridge is the oldest in Rome; it was built in 62 B.C. by Lucius Fabricius, the official in charge of road maintenance, and bears his name on its arches.

TIBER ISLAND

On the occasion of a plague in 291 B.C., the Roman Senate dispatched an embassy to the famous sanctuary of Aesculapius, the Greek god of healing, at Epidaurus. The serpent which they brought back left the ship on the voyage up the Tiber, and swam up the stream to the island, where it rested, thus determining the site for a temple to Aesculapius. At low tide the ancient travertine structure which gave the island the appearance of a ship is still to be seen, and at its southern extremity a relief showing a bust of Aesculapius and a serpent is preserved. This temple of Aesculapius was the ancient predecessor of the present Hospice and Church of S. Bartolomeo. The church was founded by the German Emperor Otto III *c.* 1000; its interior has fourteen ancient columns.

Proceeding further from the island to the right bank, on the Ponte Cestio, we see in the Tiber at our left the *Ponte Rotto,* the remains of the first Roman stone bridge over the Tiber, built between 181 and 179 B.C., repeatedly restored, for the last time by Gregory XIII, and finally swept away by the water in 1598.

Across the bridge, we continue left along the Tiber bank, turn right into the Via Dei Vascellari, and follow it to the *Church of S. Cecilia in Trastevere.* Originally the remains of the martyr saint of music were deposited in the catacombs of Callistus (p. 96); in the 9th century they were brought to the church which had been first founded, according to legend, in the saint's house. The forecourt has an ancient marble vase. The three-aisled church has been restored in modern times. At the left of the entrance is the tomb of Cardinal Fortiguerra by the Florentine Mino da Fiesole. The high altar is by Arnolfo di Cambio, the builder of the first parts of Florence Cathedral (1293). In its shrine, the recumbent statue of the beheaded St. Cecilia, by Stefano Maderna (1599). In the tribune are mosaics of the 9th century: at the center, Christ enthroned; on the left, St. Paul, St. Agatha, Pope Paschal I, the builder of the church, holding the model, his head surrounded by the square halo of the living; on the right, Sts. Peter, Valerian, and Cecilia; beneath, twelve lambs, and verses on the saint and on the building of the church. In the sacristy, a relief of the Madonna by Mino da Fiesole. Stairs at the right of the apse lead to the sepulchral chapel of St. Cecilia, which has remains of antique Roman buildings.

Via dei Genovesi, next to the church, leads to Viale del Re; we turn right in the direction of the Tiber, and reach, on the left, the *Church of S. Crisogono.* The three-aisled basilica, with twenty-two ancient granite columns, was built in the 12th century. The mosaic of the apse, by Pietro Cavallini, a contemporary of Giotto, shows the Madonna enthroned between Sts. Crisogonus and James. The sacristy gives access to excavations in the lower church, which dates back to the 5th century. In the right aisle, 11th-century frescoes with scenes from the lives of Sts. Benedict and Sylvester.

Via della Lungaretta at the right of the church takes us quickly to the *Church of S. Maria in Trastevere,* first built, according to legend, on the spot where an oil well issued forth at the birth of Christ. Its present form is of the 12th century; the vestibule dates from 1702. The mosaics on the pediment are modern; those on the façade date from the 12th century and show the Madonna, with the small figures of Pope Innocent II and Pope Innocent III at her sides, and ten virgins, some with lighted and some with extinguished lamps (the wise and the foolish). The three-aisled interior has twenty-two ancient columns. The rich ceiling dates from 1617; at its center, an Assumption by Domenichino. Near the entrance at the right, a marble tabernacle by Mino da Fiesole. The mosaics on the arch and the vaulting of the apse date from 1139-1153. Those on the arch show the Cross with Alpha and Omega between the seven candelabra and the symbols of the evangelists, Isaiah and Jeremiah to the right and left; those in the apse, Christ and Mary between saints, with Pope Innocent II holding a model of the church. Those below, showing thirteen lambs and scenes from the Life of the Virgin, are by Cavallini. To the right of the choir is the tomb of Cardinal Armellini, treasurer of Leo X, by Andrea Sansovino (1524).

We proceed a few steps farther along the Via della Lungaretta; then, right, to the Via della Scala, from which, to the left, the winding Via del Cedro leads to a steep staircase. Ascending this we arrive at the Spanish Academy of Painting and the *Church of S. Pietro in Montorio* nearby. This church was built in 1472 by Ferdinand and Isabella, the Spanish King and Queen who gave Spain its new glory, on the site where, according to Medieval legend, the Apostle Peter was crucified under Nero. The first chapel on the right has a Scourging of Christ by Sebastiano del Piombo (1518), a pupil of Michelangelo; the remaining frescoes in the chapel are also his. The second chapel on the right has, on its vaulting, a Coronation of Mary,

S. MARIA IN TRASTEVERE

and the Four Christian Virtues, by Peruzzi. Beatrice Cenci
is buried under the steps of the high altar. To escape the
infamous inclinations of her father, she conspired with her
brother to murder him, and was in consequence executed
in 1599. The fifth chapel on the left has a Baptism of
Christ by Daniele da Volterra, also a pupil of Michelangelo. In the second chapel on the left, the architecture,
and the reliefs, showing the course of human life, are by
Bernini.

In the court adjoining the church is the famous *Tem-
pietto of Bramante,* built in 1499-1502 on the spot where
legend placed Peter's cross. This is a circular building

of severe Doric style, expressing the Renaissance ideal of architectural perfection.

The terrace in front of the church affords a magnificent, sweeping view of Rome. In the foreground, to the extreme right, near the Tiber, is the Basilica of S. Paolo fuori le Mura (p. 90). Then, near the Porta S. Paolo, the Pyramid of Cestius (p. 90). There follow the churches of the Aventine (p. 86). Beyond them are the Alban Hills and Monte Cavo. Then, above the Palatine, the statues of the Lateran Basilica become visible, also the Colosseum (p. 33), the arches of the Basilica of Constantine (p. 32), the Capitoline hill, and the Church of Aracoeli (p. 119). Near the cypresses, the palace of the Quirinal (p. 116), and in front of it the Column of Trajan, and the Church of Gesù. Farther left in the foreground, near the Tiber, is the Palazzo Farnese, and, to the right of it, a section of the Pantheon dome and the Column of Marcus Aurelius. Beyond are the green gardens of the Pincio and the Villa Medici. Farther to the left, in the distance, is Mount Soracte. In the extreme left foreground are the Castel S. Angelo and the dome of St. Peter's.

We ascend the Via Garibaldi to the *Acqua Paola*, an ornamental fountain which dates back to Emperor Trajan. Its water is brought from Lago Bracciano, a distance of over 30 miles. The handsome fountain was built under Paul V in 1612 by Fontana and Maderna.

From the Acqua Paola the Via Garibaldi leads to the Porta S. Pancrazio. Nearby, on Via Angelo Masina within the wall, is the American Academy in Rome, for scholars and students of classical antiquity and of the fine arts.

Via S. Pancrazio continues to the entrance of the magnificent *Villa Doria Pamphili* with its large park, the property of Prince Doria. The Villa was laid out by Algardi in 1650 for Camillo Pamphili, nephew of Innocent X. It is not open to the public. Some steps farther is the modest church of S. Pancrazio, first founded *c.* 500.

We return on Via S. Pancrazio, pass through the Porta S. Pancrazio, and follow Via Garibaldi until we reach,

on the left, the entrance to the *Passegiata del Gianicolo.*
Here there are numerous busts of distinguished Italians
of modern times, monuments of Giuseppe Garibaldi and
his wife, and a magnificent view of Rome. At the northern end of the park is the so-called Oak of Tasso. Here
the poet of the great epic, *Jerusalem Delivered,* (who died
in the nearby monastery of St. Onofrio), used to take his
rest.

Below is the *Church of S. Onofrio,* built in 1419. The
vestibule has beautiful frescoes with scenes from the life
of St. Jerome by Domenichino. The tribune has scenes
from the life of the Virgin, those below the cornice by
Peruzzi, and those above by Pinturicchio.

A few steps from the church along the steep Salita di
S. Onofrio bring us to a large stairway leading down to
the Tiber bank, on the right. We descend, and five minutes' walk to the right on the Via della Lungara at the
bottom brings us to the garden gate of the *Villa Farnesina,*
on the left. This was built in 1509-1511 by the rich banker
and art patron Agostino Chigi after plans of Baldassare
Peruzzi. Chigi gave large drinking parties in the garden,
and to top his extravagance threw the valuable golden
goblets that had been used into the Tiber—where they
were caught in concealed nets and recovered.

The entrance hall of the Farnesina has the famous
ceiling frescoes illustrating the story of Cupid and Psyche,
from the *Golden Ass* by Apuleius. These were executed in
1516-1518 from cartoons of Raphael by his pupils Giulio
Romano, Francesco Penni, and Giovanni da Udine. The
room adjoining on the left has Raphael's Galatea, painted
in 1514. To the left is Sebastiano del Piombo's Polyphemus,
spoiled by restoration. On the ceiling are configurations,
the zodiac, and the seven planetary deities by Baldassare
Peruzzi. The stories from Ovid's *Metamorphoses* in the
lunettes were painted by del Piombo in 1511.

The principal hall of the upper floor has architectural
paintings with Roman views and a frieze with scenes from
Greek mythology by Peruzzi. In what used to be the second
bedchamber is the marriage of Alexander the Great and

Roxane by Sodoma (1511-1512). On the exit wall, the family of Darius, also by Sodoma.

In the continuation of the Via della Lungara to the square on the right, a fine old magnolia tree marks the entrance to the Museo Torlonia (closed to visitors) which possesses ancient statues and reliefs.

We end our walk by passing through the Porta Settimiana and, a few streets to the left, to the Ponte Sisto, to recross the Tiber.

FROM THE AVENTINE TO S. PAOLO FUORI LE MURA

Opposite the Palatine the Clivo dei Publici ascends to the quiet Via S. Sabina. Here, immediately to the right, are the grounds of the Parco dell'Aventino, with fine views. Adjacent, restored to its Early Christian and Medieval character, is the Dominican *Monastery Church of S. Sabina*. The church was first founded in 425, renewed in the 9th century, and bestowed on St. Dominic for his order by Pope Honorius III in the 13th century. Its famous cypress-wood doors of the 5th century contain scenes from the Old and New Testaments in eighteen panels; with Early Christian sarcophagi and mosaics, this door is the most venerable monument of Early Christian art. The interior, with its twenty-four Corinthian columns and open timber roof, illustrates the basilica type of the 5th century, but little altered by later additions. Over the door of the entrance wall is a mosaic of 480 recording the name of the donor of the church. On the left is the figure of the Church of Jewish Christians, on the right of Gentile Christians. In the right aisle, the Chapel of S. Giacinto, with frescoes of scenes from the life of the saint by the brothers Zuccari, second half of the 16th century. In the left aisle, the Cappella d'Elci contains the Madonna del Rosario with Sts. Dominic and Catherine, a 17th-century masterpiece by Sassoferrato.

Immediately to the right is the *Church of S. Alessio*. The monastery with its fine colonnade is now an institution for the blind.

PYRAMID OF CESTIUS AND PORTA S. PAOLO

The adjoining *Piazza dei Cavalieri di Malta* owes its architectural adornment to the great Venetian engraver, G. B. Piranesi (1765). No. 40 is the entrance to the Maltese Priorate; through an aperture in the door above the keyhole, a famous view of St. Peter's dome.

Opposite, to the left, the austere modern Church and the impressive international Benedictine College of S. Anselmo. At the left of S. Anselmo the Via di S. Anselmo leads down to the Piazza Albania, at the left of which a substantial part of the so-called Servian wall is preserved. This does not, however, date from the early regal period, as was formerly believed, but from the fortifications of 380 B.C., after the Gallic invasion. From the piazza, the Via S. Saba mounts to the right to the *Church of S. Saba,* named after a Cappadocian monk (439-532). In the lower church is the Oratory of St. Silvia, mother of Pope Gregory the Great. The upper church has fourteen ancient columns and an open timber roof. There is a large Roman sarcophagus with nuptial scenes in the vestibule.

From the Piazza Albania, the Viale Piramide Cestia leads to the *Porta S. Paolo*, called Porta Ostiensis in antiquity, because through it passed the road to Ostia (p. 162). The gate is part of the renovation of the Aurelian Wall by Emperor Honorius in 402 A.D.

During the Empire, Rome had far outgrown the walls erected after the Gallic invasions and had become an open city. But when, after 271, Germanic tribes invaded Upper Italy, pressed forward to Umbria, and threatened Rome itself, Emperor Aurelian erected the wall called by his name. It had a length of more than eleven miles, 383 towers, and sixteen gates.

Near the Porta S. Paolo is the *Pyramid of Cestius*. According to its inscription, the Praetor and Tribune of the People, Caius Cestius, provided by will in 12 B.C. that the tomb be erected in the Egyptian fashion within 330 days after his death. The pyramid is 120 ft. high, but part of it is still under ground.

On the city side of the Porta S. Paolo, to the left, Via Caio Cestio leads to the entrance of the *Protestant Cemetery*, where many English, Germans, Scandinavians, Russians, and Americans lie buried. Above, on the wall, a monument containing the heart of Shelley, who was drowned in the Gulf of Spezia in 1822; Lord Byron had Shelley's body burned on a pyre.

Farther to the west rises *Monte Testaccio*, a hill composed wholly of ancient shards of wine and oil vessels from ancient Roman transports and warehouses on the Tiber.

In front of Porta S. Paolo, on the left, is the station of the electric railway to Ostia Antica and the Lido (p. 162).

A half-hour's walk on the Via Ostiense brings us to S. *Paolo fuori le Mura*, the greatest of the Roman pilgrimage churches after St. Peter's. Emperor Constantine erected a church over the grave of St. Paul, but the present basilica dates back to the foundation of Emperors Valentinian, Theodosius, and Arcadius (A.D. 386). It received its rich mosaic decorations with the aid of Empress Galla Placidia, under Pope Leo I in the 5th century. In the 9th cen-

S. PAOLO FUORI LE MURA

S. PAOLO FUORI LE MURA. CLOISTER

tury, church and monastery were plundered by the Saracens, and then made into a fortress. In 1823 the nave and aisles were destroyed by fire; the church was rebuilt in the first half of the 19th century on the ancient plans.

The church is entered through a modern colonnaded court. The principal façade, with modern mosaics, looks toward the Tiber. The effect of the interior is overwhelming, despite the chilly splendor of the modern restoration. As no other church interior in Rome, it conveys the quiet dignity of a Roman basilica, such as the Basilica Julia in the Forum (p. 15) and Trajan's Basilica Ulpia (p. 30) must once have possessed. The interior space (400 by 200 ft.; 75 ft. high) is divided into five aisles by a forest of eighty columns connected by round arches. The best view is from the end of the second aisle on the right, near the entrance, and it is best seen in the late afternoon, when the fading light dims the brilliance of the modern marble.

A modern mosaic frieze over the columns of the three central aisles and in the transept contains likenesses of all 261 Popes down to Pius XII. The triumphal arch has the restored mosaics of Galla Placidia: at the center, a medallion of Christ; next, the symbols of the evangelists; beneath, the twenty-four elders of the Apocalypse; below, right and left, the Apostles Peter and Paul on blue ground.

The tabernacle of the high altar is a masterpiece of Tuscan art of about 1285. The Easter candelabrum in the right transept with scenes from the life of Christ and animals amidst foliage belongs to the 12th century. In the apse is a vast mosaic by Venetian artists of about 1220: Christ between four apostles, and, in miniature at his feet, Pope Honorius III. Underneath is the Cross, the symbols of the Passion, two angels, and the apostles chanting the Gloria. On the right of the niche is John the Evangelist, blessing a small kneeling figure of Pope John XXII.

From the right transept we enter the magnificent cloister (first half of the 13th century) with numerous remains of ancient inscriptions and sculptures.

A few minutes' walk on Via Ostiense beyond S. Paolo brings us to the Via Laurentina on the left, which offers

a rewarding walk to the Trappist *Abbey of Tre Fontane.*
It is named for the three springs which, legend says,
sprang up at the execution of the Apostle Paul, when
his head bounded on the ground three times after it was
struck off. The main church, SS. Vincenzo e Anastasio,
an antique, columned basilica, is in the monastery court.
The round church at its right, built in 1582, is called S.
Maria Scala Coeli because here, according to legend, there
appeared to St. Bernard the heavenly ladder upon which
those redeemed by his prayers were carried to heaven
by angels. The third church, at the back, S. Paolo alle Tre
Fontane, contains the three springs and a fine ancient
mosaic from Ostia showing the four seasons.

Nearby are the unfinished grounds planned for a world
fair after World War II.

FROM THE CHURCHES OF THE CAELIUS TO VIA APPIA
AND THE CATACOMBS

From the Arch of Constantine (p. 35), the Via S. Gregorio
runs parallel to the slope of the Palatine. On its left is the
Antiquarium, a garden and storehouse containing antiquities found in the area of Rome. Next, on the left, the
Clivo di Scauro leads through a brick arch to the picturesque square with the *Church of SS. Giovanni e Paolo,*
founded about 400 on the site of the house of the two
saints, who were high officials at the court and suffered
martyrdom under Emperor Julian the Apostate. The Campanile, the exterior with its gallery of small columns, and
the vestibule with its two lions date from the 12th century; the interior, redecorated in the Baroque style, is un-
interesting. It is, however, worth while to descend, at the
end of the right aisle, to the excavated remains of the
Roman house. In addition to ancient frescoes, its rooms
contain Early Christian examples also: Moses at Mount
Horeb; Moses receiving the Tables of the Law; scenes
of martyrdom. The most important picture is an ancient
fresco of the 2nd century A.D.—an Island of the Blessed
with two figures on the sea.

S. STEFANO ROTONDO

The Via di S. Paolo della Croce leads on to the Arch
of the Consuls Dolabella and Silanus which dates from
10 A.D. Immediately to the right, the Piazza della Navicella, named after a fountain in the shape of a small
marble ship, copied after an ancient piece which was
probably a votive offering after a perilous sea voyage.

In the piazza, the *Church of S. Maria in Domnica* or
della Navicella. This is a very ancient church, rebuilt by
Pope Paschal in 817. The interior has three aisles and
eighteen granite columns. The much restored mosaics of
817-823 show, on the triumphal arch, Christ between two
angels and the apostles, and, beneath, the two Sts. John;
in the apse, Pope Paschal kissing the feet of the Madonna.

Adjacent is the entrance to the *Villa Celimontana*, a
public park with charming paths and a beautiful view of
the Baths of Caracalla and the Alban hills.

From Piazza della Navicella the Via di S. Stefano Rotondo leads to the *Church of S. Stefano Rotondo;* the
entrance is at No. 7. Built under Pope Simplicius in the
5th century, this is an impressive circular edifice with

twenty-two columns in its inner circle and forty-four in its outer. The supporting wall of the roof with its lofty columns borne by three arches dates from the 9th century. A mosaic of the 7th century in the small apse of the outer ambulatory shows Christ on the Cross.

We retrace our way to Via di S. Gregorio. A few steps to the left from our starting point bring us to the façade of the *Church of S. Gregorio Magno* (1633); the oldest church on this site was built by Pope Gregory the Great in 575, in his father's house. The forecourt has fine tombs. In the interior, sixteen ancient columns. To the right of the right aisle is a small room from the house of St. Gregory; it contains an interesting antique marble chair.

Left of the church are three chapels connected by a portico: on the right, the Chapel of St. Silvia, mother of Gregory the Great; on the left, the Chapel of St. Barbara; in the center, the Chapel of St. Andrew. In its interior, on the right, the martyrdom of St. Andrew by Domenichino, and on the left, St. Andrew on the way to execution perceiving the cross, by Guido Reni.

Via di S. Gregorio leads on to the obelisk which the Italians brought from Aksum after the Abyssinian War in 1937. From here we follow the Viale Guido Bacelli to the *Terme di Caracalla* which tower on the right. These were begun by Septimius Severus in 206 and opened to the public by his son Caracalla in 217; they continued in use until 537, when the East Goths destroyed the aqueducts in the Campagna which fed them.

The complex of the Baths occupies an area of 360 sq. yds.; the building itself measures 720 by 375 ft. The rooms were constructed with enormous arches and richly furnished with works of art; they are said to have accommodated 1600 bathers simultaneously. The baths are entered through the spacious hall of the *frigidarium*, with a swimming pool of cold water. On either side are small rooms for undressing. The great central hall with four large basins for lukewarm water at the corner piers has gymnasiums adjoining it on either side. The round hall opposite the entrance, 115 ft. in diameter, contained the

BATHS OF CARACALLA: FRIGIDARIUM

steam bath. The bath house was surrounded by landscaped gardens and fields for gymnastic games. The large apses in the enclosing wall were lecture halls. The chambers opposite the entrance contained the water reservoirs. In front of them, benches for spectators of the athletic displays.

Issuing from the Baths, we turn right to the Piazzale Numa Pompilio; at the intersection, the right fork is the Via di Porta S. Sebastiano, which continues beyond the gate as Via Appia.

On the right is the quiet Church of S. Cesareo, and immediately following, the house of Cardinal Bessarion of Trebizond, one of the first humanists of the 15th century, who labored for the union of the Greek and Roman Churches at the Council of Florence in 1439.

Further on, to the left, No. 12, is the *Tomb of the Scipios,* one of the greatest families of Rome, to which the conquerors of Carthage (202 and 147 B.C.) and of Antiochus of Syria (190 B.C.) belonged. Behind it is the

DOMINE QUO VADIS

excellently preserved Columbarium of Pomponius Hylas, a freedman of the time of Nero; this is decorated with charming frescoes.

Some minutes further on, shortly before the Porta S. Sebastiano, the so-called Arch of Drusus. This is not a triumphal arch, and has nothing to do with Drusus, but is the arch of an aqueduct of the 3rd century A.D.

The city gate, Porta S. Sebastiano, is much as Emperor Honorius' reconstruction left it. Next, after the pass under the Rome-Civitavecchia-Pisa railway, the slope above affords a splendid view of the city, protected by the Aurelian Wall, as in antiquity.

About ten minutes further, on the left, is the small church, *Domine Quo Vadis,* ("Lord, whither goest Thou?"). It was here, according to legend, that Christ encountered Peter in flight from a martyr's death. Upon Peter's question, "Lord, whither goest Thou?" Christ replied, "I come to be crucified again." Thereupon Peter returned to Rome.

Some twenty-five minutes out of the Porta S. Sebastiano, at No. 110 of the Via Appia, by the cypresses, is the entrance to the *Catacombs of S. Callisto*. Roman law prohibited burials within the city walls; hence Roman tombs are immediately outside the walls, like that of Bibulus (p. 119), or in an open field, like that of Augustus (p. 107). It was also the Roman custom to have family tombs, which extended burial to freed family slaves, as in the case of the Tomb of the Scipios (p. 94), and to provide vast undecorated repositories for those without means. Early Christianity, following Jewish tradition, rejected cremation. Hence subterranean burial places with rows of Christian graves were laid out in the easily worked volcanic rock of the outskirts of Rome. In the 3rd century the strengthened Church took charge of the administration of these mass burials. In times of persecution their concealment under ground afforded refuge. Constantine's legislation gave the Catacombs peace and security. In the 5th century they were discontinued, and burials took place in and near churches. But the memory of the martyrs buried in the Catacombs survived, and forms of special worship at specific tombs were developed. This was followed by the cult of saints and martyrs of the Medieval Church, which led to an extensive removal of the relics of martyrs to cathedrals and churches, where every altar became a reliquary. The Catacombs themselves eventually fell into oblivion, and it was only with the accidental discovery of a Catacomb in 1578 that the modern investigation of this subterranean Roman world, still far from completed, began.

Christianity had its origin among the simple folk of Palestine, and did not possess its own art. In order to adapt itself to the Greco-Roman world with its joy in form and color, it had to adopt the language of that art. Hence the art of the Catacombs forms part of the contemporary Greco-Roman art. It was only the style, however, that was borrowed; new symbolic meaning was attached to the images and motifs adopted. But with the development of the 3rd and 4th centuries, specifically

TOMB OF CAECILIA METELLA

Christian formulations of the narratives of the Old and New Testaments appear.

Of the more than forty Catacombs which have been discovered in the environs of Rome, that of Callistus is the most important. Here English-speaking monks serve as guides, and these provide brief or detailed explanations, as the visitor desires.

Five minutes farther along on the Via Appia, to the right, is the *Basilica of S. Sebastiano*, one of the seven ancient pilgrimage churches, renovated in 1612. The first chapel to the right has a stone bearing Christ's footprint, according to the Quo Vadis legend. In the first chapel on the left is a handsome statue of St. Sebastian, after a design by Bernini. The Catacombs that belong to the church are less important than those of S. Callisto.

Shortly before S. Sebastiano, the Via delle Sette Chiese diverges to the right; in it, at No. 22, on the left, are the Catacombs of Domitilla, or of Sts. Nereus and Achilleus,

which have important frescoes. In the center, the three-aisled Basilica of St. Petronilla.

Some 300 yards farther on the Via Appia and at the left, the large gateway of the *Circus of Maxentius,* dedicated in 307 A.D. to the memory of the Emperor's son Romulus who died as a youth. The Circus is 530 yds. long and accommodated 18,000 spectators; from it came the obelisk in the Piazza Navona. Next, on the ascending slope of the road, is the famous *Tomb of Caecilia Metella,* daughter-in-law of the millionaire Crassus, killed in battle against the Parthians in 53 B.C. The frieze with ox skulls and garlands also exhibits Gallic weapons, presumably because Caecilia's husband participated in Julius Caesar's campaign against the Gauls in 55 B.C. In the Middle Ages the circular structure, 65 ft. in diameter, was a stronghold of the Gaetani, the family of Pope Boniface VIII.

The most attractive part of the Via Appia begins from here: Tombs and cypresses, splendid views of the ruins and of the Alban Hills, make it well worth while to follow it for a time.

S. AGNESE FUORI LE MURA, S. COSTANZA,
S. LORENZO FUORI LE MURA

From the Porta Pia in the Aurelian Wall, built in 1561 after plans by Michelangelo, the Via Nomentana reaches, 1¼ miles from the gate, the *Church of St. Agnes Outside the Walls*. The first church of St. Agnes was built in the 4th century by Constantia, daughter of Constantine the Great, on her estate on Via Nomentana. Of this church, only a portion of the enclosing wall is preserved, adjacent to S. Costanza (see below). The present church was built by Pope Honorius I in the 7th century, over the grave of the saint. It has been repeatedly restored.

A gateway leads to a court, at the right of which a marble staircase descends to the church. The interior has three aisles with sixteen ancient columns, and over the side aisles and entrance wall a gallery with smaller columns. Under the tabernacle is the alabaster figure of St. Agnes, a pagan statue put to new use. In the apse, St. Agnes, against a resplendent gold ground, between Pope Honorius I, holding a model of the church, and Pope Symmachus. The hand of God emerges from clouds. On January 21, the Feast of St. Agnes, two lambs are offered here, and their fleeces used for pallia for archbishops of the Catholic Church. Catacombs accessible to visitors also belong to the church.

The court of St. Agnes also gives access to the round *Church of S. Costanza*, built as a mausoleum by Constantia to adjoin the former church. Twenty-four paired granite columns in the interior support a dome 74 ft. in diameter. Its abundant light contrasts with the dim, windowless ambulatory. The barrel vaults of the ambulatory have excellently preserved mosaics of Cupids at the vintage, blue against white ground. The large niche in the main axis has the monogram of Christ; the vaulting in the niche of the transverse axis has the delivery of the law and the keys to Peter. The porphyry sarcophagus of Constantia in the Vatican Museum (p. 56) came from this church. Despite its partial destruction this circular church provides an example of the art of the age of Constantine at its purest.

To reach *S. Lorenzo fuori le Mura* we start out from the Lateran. At the left of the Piazza di S. Giovanni, facing at an angle the façade of the Lateran Church, is the edifice housing the *Scala Santa,* a stairway of twenty-eight steps, which legend asserts came from the house of Pontius Pilate in Jerusalem. The stairs were brought to Rome at the end of the Crusades in the 13th century. They may be ascended on the knees only. At the top is the old private chapel of the Popes which was part of the old Lateran palace; it contains a 9th-century mosaic of Christ.

At the foot of the steps, to the right side, a tribune erected by Benedict XIV in the 18th century. The 8th-century mosaic from the dining hall of Leo III in the old Lateran palace is here restored from drawings: At the center, Christ on the heavenly mount, from which the rivers of Paradise issue, sends forth the disciples; at the left, Christ enthroned delivers the keys to Pope Sylvester and the banner to Emperor Constantine; on the right, St. Peter delivers the papal stole to Leo III, and the banner to Charlemagne.

The Piazza di Porta S. Giovanni extends in front of the niche and the Lateran. At the right, near the new gate, are preserved two cylindrical towers from the old Porta Asinaria of the Aurelian Wall, through which the East Goths under Totila treacherously made their way into the city. Beyond the street, the modern bronze monument of St. Francis of Assisi.

Further down, to the right, the Baroque façade (1743) of the *Church of S. Croce in Gerusalemme,* one of the seven pilgrimage churches. On her pilgrimage to Jerusalem in the early thirties of the 4th century, St. Helena, mother of Constantine the Great, discovered the Sepulcher and Cross of Christ. About 350 one of her grandsons erected a church within her palace for this most precious relic of Christendom. Of this oldest foundation virtually nothing remains; the Romanesque Campanile dates from 1144.

The interior is a Baroque renovation. Ancient **granite**

S. CROCE IN GERUSALEMME

columns support the nave. The vaulting of the apse has a
fresco of the school of Pinturicchio (1492)—the discovery
of the Cross by St. Helena. Beneath is the tomb of Cardinal Quiñones, the confessor of Emperor Charles V, by
Jacopo Sansovino (1536). A stair at the end of the left
aisle descends to the lower church. Here, at the altar of
the left chapel, is a fine 16th-century Pietà in relief. At
either side, 14th-century statuettes of Peter and Paul. On
the right, the Chapel of St. Helena. In the vaulting, excellently preserved mosaics, perhaps after designs by
Melozzo da Forli: At the center, Christ with the four
evangelists; in the arch over the entrance, at the left, St.
Helena with the Cross that is being adored by Cardinal
Carrajal, of the court of Alexander VI; at the right, St.
Sylvester; over the altar, Sts. Peter and Paul. The altar
statue is an ancient marble figure now representing St.
Helena.

From S. Croce we turn left at the end of the square, into the Via Eleniana, and find ourselves facing the *Porta Maggiore*. According to the inscription on the upper part of the attic the magnificent double gate was built in 52 A.D. by Emperor Claudius as an aqueduct to bring the waters of Aqua Claudia, and above, the waters of the Anio Novus, into the city. Aurelian incorporated the gate into his wall.

Before the gate rises a curiosity: the *Tomb of Marcus Vergilius Eurysaces*, the baker. With typically Roman realism, the tomb imitates grain measures piled up in a system of vertical and horizontal cylinders. The frieze above depicts the manufacture and sale of bread.

Passing through the gate and following the Via Prenestina on the left, we come, shortly before the railway bridge, to the entrance of the *Basilica di Porta Maggiore*, an underground structure accidentally discovered in 1916. The interior, 20 by 30 ft., is divided into three aisles by pillars; its ceiling is richly decorated in stucco. In the nave, Ganymede, the favorite of Zeus, is borne up to heaven by a daimon. In the apse of the nave, the Greek poetess Sappho descends into the sea, where she is received by tritons. Apollo, on the opposite bank, welcomes Sappho; behind Apollo is Phaon, lover of Sappho, who awaits eternal union with her in the beyond. These and the numerous other stucco reliefs have been interpreted as symbols of immortality pertaining to some Orphic-Pythagorean religious community of the 1st century A.D. The basilica would then have been their meeting house.

Following, on the city side, the Viale Giovanni Giolitti to the left, we soon come to the mighty vaults of the ruins of the so-called *Temple of Minerva Medica*. This decagonal structure of the 3rd century A.D. was probably a nymphaeum, or fountain room.

A few steps to the right, the Porta Prenestina leads to the railway underpass; we follow the Aurelian Wall to the left to Porta S. Lorenzo, and then to the Porta Tiburtina. In 5 B.C., Augustus built here an arch over the road leading to Tivoli, to carry the aqueducts of Marcia, Tepula,

PORTA MAGGIORE. TOMB OF M. V. EURYSACES

and Julia. The arch is now buried deep in the ground; the upper portion of the double attic has Augustus' inscription.

We return to the Porta S. Lorenzo and from here follow the Via Tiburtina straight ahead to *S. Lorenzo fuori le Mura*. This too is one of the seven pilgrimage churches of Rome. It was seriously damaged in World War II, but is now fortunately restored. The present church goes back to a new construction of Pope Honorius III, which replaced an older church of the age of Constantine.

The paintings on the façade, with figures of the builders and donors of the church, were made in 1864. The front part of the interior is divided into three aisles by twenty-two unequal ancient columns. Handsome, 12th-century mosaic floor. At the entrance is a fine Roman sarcophagus, depicting a wedding. In the nave the two pulpits—for the Epistle on the right and the Gospel on the left—and the Easter candelabrum all date from the 12th century. At the end of the left aisle, stairs descend to the Church of

S. LORENZO FUORI LE MURA

Pope Pelagius II, built in 578, which is 10 ft. lower. The aisles had been covered up, and were excavated after 1870. Twelve beautiful antique columns support the entablature composed of ancient fragments. The triumphal arch has 6th-century mosaics depicting Christ and saints. The tabernacle dates from 1148. In the back part is the simple tomb of Pope Pius IX (died 1878). The sacristy at the end of the right aisle of the front part of the basilica gives access to the beautiful Romanesque cloister of the 12th century.

Adjoining S. Lorenzo is the extensive modern cemetery, Campo Verano.

SQUARES, FOUNTAINS, PALACES

No CITY in the world can vie with Rome in wealth of individual public squares. The alternation of hill and valley characteristic of the city afforded architects rich scope for their fancy. With two of these great creations, the Piazza di S. Pietro (p. 42) and the Piazza di S. Ignazio (p. 76), we have already become familiar.

We begin our new tour with the *Piazza del Popolo,* dominated by the great obelisk at its center. According to the inscription upon its base, this was brought to Rome from Heliopolis in Lower Egypt by Augustus in 10 B.C., set up in the Circus Maximus, and dedicated to the sun. Its hieroglyphics yield the name of Rameses II, of the 13th century B.C. It was erected in its present position by Sixtus V. Including base and cross, its height is 119 ft.

Toward the north the piazza is bounded by the Porta del Popolo. This portal in the Aurelian Wall was decorated on the interior side by Bernini in 1655 for the ceremonial entry of Queen Christina of Sweden. Beyond the gate, the Via Flaminia, the pilgrimage road to Rome before the construction of railways, leads to the Ponte Milvio across the Tiber, and thence onward to the north.

To the right of the Porta del Popolo, facing into the square, the *Church of S. Maria del Popolo,* built by Sixtus IV in 1472-1477 to replace an older structure which was erected, according to legend, to exorcise the evil spirit of Emperor Nero living in an oak tree. The interior, nave and two aisles, is rich in frescoes and monuments, mainly from the 15th century. The first chapel on the right contains an altarpiece and frescoes by Pinturicchio; the third

PORTA DEL POPOLO

chapel is similarly decorated by Pinturicchio (approximately 1504-1507). Giovanni, Duke of Gandia, the favorite son of the Borgia Pope Alexander VI, is buried in the second chapel to the right of the choir; he was mysteriously murdered in 1497 and his body found in the Tiber. The choir contains very beautiful ceiling frescoes by Pinturicchio (1508-1509): The Coronation of Mary, The Four Evangelists, and The Four Church Fathers, Gregory, Ambrose, Jerome, Augustine. The second chapel of the left aisle, counting from the entrance, is the Chigi Chapel, built and decorated with mosaics in 1516 by the rich banker Agostino Chigi after cartoons by Raphael. In the center of the dome, God the Father surrounded by angels; in the second row, the Genius of the sun and the seven planets, surrounded by the signs of the zodiac and by angels. In the niches, four statues of prophets; Jonah, at the left of the altar, after a design of Raphael.

The square as an architectural whole, with its delimitations to east and west by walls and statues, was created in 1809-1814 by Valadier, at Napoleon's request.

Opposite the Porta del Popolo, three streets radiate from

ARA PACIS AUGUSTAE

the piazza. Adjoining the right one of the twin churches, S. Maria dei Miracoli, the Via di Ripetta leads off to the right, and in five minutes we reach the *Mausoleum of Augustus* on our left. This is a circular structure 292 ft. in diameter and 144 ft. high, buried deep in the ground. Its summit was originally crowned by a statue of the Emperor, and the entrance flanked by two obelisks. Of these, one now stands on the Piazza del Quirinale (p. 116), and the other behind S. Maria Maggiore (p. 71). The ashes of the Emperor, who died 14 A.D., and of the numerous members of his family who predeceased him, were deposited in the Mausoleum; only a few inscriptions survive.

Opposite the Mausoleum of Augustus, by the Tiber, the *Ara Pacis Augustae* has been reconstructed in a special pavilion. The Ara Pacis was an altar of peace, dedicated by Augustus in 9 B.C. after the wars he waged in various parts of the world. The altar stood at the center

PIAZZA COLONNA

of a small court, the marble walls of which were richly decorated with reliefs on both their inner and outer surfaces. The entire monument lay 23 ft. under the modern street level, beneath the Palazzo Fiano, in a lateral street of the Corso. Excavations on the spot have been carried on since the Renaissance, and finds made their way to various museums of Europe. In 1937-1938 the Italian government carried out an extremely difficult but definitive excavation. The finds, old and new, together with necessary additions to supplement missing parts, have been united in the present reconstruction. The simplicity of the structure, the balanced composition of its ornamentation, the perfection of its carving, and the dignity of the numerous figures represented in procession make the Ara Pacis the noblest Augustan work preserved to us.

The main entrance is reached by a stair. The door is framed by pillars and elaborate foliage ornamentation, and above, a relief; to the right, Aeneas, as founder of Roman rule in Latium, is shown sacrificing a sow to the Penates. On the exterior wall, to the left of the door, a relief: the goddess Tellus as symbol of the fruitful earth, surrounded by the divine spirits of the air—on the left the goddess of terrestrial winds upon a swan, and on the right the goddess of sea winds upon a sea-dragon. The figured frieze on the longitudinal walls, moving towards the entrance, depicts the festive procession when Augustus laid the corner-stone of the sanctuary in 13 B.C.; it was completed in 9 B.C. In the interior of the enclosing walls rises the richly ornamented altar.

A few steps farther on bring us to the Ponte Cavour over the Tiber. At its left rises the magnificent Palazzo Borghese, completed by Paul V. Within the palace is an imposing court containing three ancient colossal statues.

The central street of the three radiating from the Piazza del Popolo is called Via del Corso, after the horse-races which traditionally ran its length from the Piazza del Popolo to the Piazza Venezia. A few steps along the Via del Corso take us to Nos. 517 and 519, the Palazzo Sanseverino, formerly Rondanini, which contained the Pietà Rondanini, a late work of Michelangelo, now in No. 2 Via Neola. Five minutes' further walk brings us to a view, between modern buildings to the right, of the Mausoleum of Augustus. Then follows the *Church of S. Carlo al Corso*, with its columned façade, built in 1690. The church is dedicated to the two great bishops of Milan, St. Ambrose and St. Carlo Borromeo. Over the high altar the masterpiece of Carlo Maratta: The Madonna commending St. Carlo Borromeo to Christ. A few steps beyond the street crossing and to the right is the gloomy Palazzo Ruspoli, by Ammanati (1586). Next, again to the right, an elongated square, containing the *Church of S. Lorenzo in Lucina* with its colonnaded vestibule. By the second pillar to the right in the interior, the tomb of Nicolas Poussin, the great landscape painter, which was commissioned by the French poet Chateaubriand. Next to the right, opposite the much frequented Café Aragno, is the Palazzo Verospi, now occupied by the Credito Italiano. Here Shelley lived in 1819, when he wrote his *Prometheus* and *Beatrice Cenci*.

SCALA DI SPAGNA

We have now arrived at the *Piazza Colonna*, with the *Column of Marcus Aurelius* at its center. The column, consisting of twenty-eight drums and rising to a height of 97 ft., is modeled after the Column of Trajan (p. 30), and its reliefs in twenty-three spirals, originally painted, depict the campaigns of Emperor Marcus Aurelius, the philosopher, against the Marcomanni and Sarmatians on the Danube in 171-175 A.D. In place of the Emperor's statue, which has disappeared, Pope Sixtus V crowned the column in 1589 with a bronze statue of St. Paul.

To the right of the column, the large Palazzo Chigi, now occupied by the Italian Ministry of Foreign Affairs, completed by Maderna. Behind the column, the Palazzo del Sindacato della Stampa, which has a hall containing sixteen ancient columns from Veii.

To the right of this palazzo a street leads to the *Piazza di Montecitorio*. Here, on the right, the Palazzo di Monte-

VILLA MEDICI. GARDEN FRONT

citorio, now seat of the Italian Parliament, designed by
Bernini in 1650. In front of it is a much restored obelisk
with an inscription of Psammetichus II, King of Egypt in
the 6th century B.C. This obelisk originally served as a sun
dial, and was brought to Rome by Augustus.

As we proceed further on the Via del Corso, we reach,
at the right corner of the square, Palazzo Ferraioli. We
follow the narrow Via di Pietra by its side and reach, after
a few steps, the Piazza di Pietra. Here, a magnificent row
of Corinthian columns about 40 ft. high, which belong to
the *Hadrianeum*, the Temple of the deified Emperor
Hadrian, 2nd century A.D. Also preserved and visible is
the platform on which the temple was erected. Originally,
the front façade had eight columns. The reliefs with figures of the Roman provinces, now in the court of the
Palazzo dei Conservatori (p. 146), derive from this temple.
The building houses at present the Exchange.

We return to the Via del Corso. Proceeding further,

111

palace follows palace. First on the left is the austere Palazzo Sciarra-Colonna, built at the beginning of the 17th century. Next on the left is the fanciful façade of the Church of S. Marcello, built by Fontana in 1708. At the right, the small Church of S. Maria in Via Lata, an old foundation beneath which are the remains of an ancient building. At the end of the left aisle is a sepulchral chapel of relatives of Napoleon. Next to this church is the Palazzo Doria with its fine colonnaded court, executed by a follower of Bernini. Its gallery has a fine portrait of Pope Innocent X (Pamphili) by Velasquez.

Opposite, the modern façade of the Palazzo Odescalchi, adjoining which is the Palazzo Salviati, whose handsome façade was designed by Rainaldi. At the end of the Corso on the right, its main façade facing the Piazza Venezia (p. 117), is the Palazzo Bonaparte. Here lived Napoleon's mother Laetitia, and from its corner balcony she watched the street life of Rome.

From the Piazza del Popolo, the Via del Babuino leads to the left to the *Piazza di Spagna,* one of the most magnificent in Rome. The piazza is dominated by the incomparably vivid Spanish Steps, constructed in 1721-1725 by Specchi and De Sanctis upon the orders of the French ambassador to the Vatican. Beneath the staircase with its flower stands is the fountain in the shape of a boat fitted with cannon: La Barcaccia, by Pietro Bernini, the father of the great Lorenzo Bernini. To the south of the fountain, in front of the palace of the Spanish ambassador to the Vatican, the Column of the Immacolata, erected by Pius IX. At its short southern end the piazza is bounded by the Palazzo di Propaganda Fide, erected by Gregory XV as a school for training missionaries of the Catholic faith. The short façade is by Bernini, the long façade in the Via di Propaganda Fide is by Borromini.

Ascending the Spanish Steps we find, on the right, the house in which the English poet Keats died on February 4, 1821. The house contains a small museum and library in his and Shelley's memory. From above, the Spanish Steps are dominated by SS. *Trinità dei Monti,* built by Charles

PIAZZA DEL QUIRINALE

VIII of France in 1495 and restored in 1816. The altar fresco in the second chapel on the left has a Descent from the Cross by Daniele da Volterra; the third chapel on the right has an Assumption by the same artist.

Proceeding from SS. Trinità dei Monti further to the left, we find ourselves in front of the *Villa Medici.* The villa, built in 1574, later came into the possession of the Medici, and in 1803, Napoleon made it the seat of the French Academy of Art. Many fine reliefs are built into the garden façade. The view of Rome as far as St. Peter's, through the evergreens on the square in front of the villa, is famous.

The broad avenue continues to the Casino Valadier (café and restaurant) and to the terrace of the Pincio above the Piazza del Popolo. The grounds were laid out by Valadier, upon orders of Napoleon. The obelisk at the center is from the tomb which Emperor Hadrian erected

FONTANA DI TREVI

in front of the Porta Maggiore (p. 102) to his beautiful favorite Antinoüs, who drowned himself in the Nile. Busts of famous Italians are placed along the walks. A bridge connects the Pincio with the Villa Borghese (p. 155).

We return, past the Villa Medici and SS. Trinità dei Monti, to the Via Sistina, which descends to the *Piazza Barberini*. In its center, the *Fontana del Tritone,* one of the most brilliant creations of Lorenzo Bernini (1640). The triton is shown blowing the lofty spray out of a seashell. Adjoining the piazza is the massive Palazzo Barberini, built by Pope Urban VIII for his family. The building was started in 1624 by Maderna and completed by Bernini. The principal façade is in the Via Quattro Fontane.

The Via Vittorio Veneto runs left from the Piazza Barberini. This is the principal thoroughfare for fashionable foreigners and has many hotels. On the right it passes the former Palazzo Margherita, now part of the American embassy, and runs on to the Porta Pinciana, opposite the entrance to the Villa Borghese (p. 155).

PALAZZO VENEZIA

We proceed from the Piazza Barberini past the Palazzo
Barberini up the Via Barberini to the right, to the *Piazza
di S. Bernardo*. At the right of the intersection is the
Fontanone dell'Acqua Felice, designed by Fontana in
1587 as a memorial of the aqueduct from the Alban hills,
constructed by Sixtus V. The colossal figure of Moses,
artistically unsuccessful, was inspired by Michelangelo's
Moses in the Church of S. Pietro in Vincoli (p. 69). The
relief on the left shows Gideon, that on the right Aaron
leading the thirsting Israelites to the miraculous water.

Across from the fountain, on the corner of Via XX Settembre, is the *Church of S. Maria della Vittoria,* designed
by Maderna (1605). The name is derived from a legend
according to which an image of the Virgin decided the
victory of the Catholic army of Emperor Ferdinand II
over the Protestants at Prague in 1620. The second chapel
on the right in the interior has an altarpiece and frescoes
by Domenichino. The fourth chapel on the left contains
Bernini's famous group of St. Teresa: an angel aiming an
arrow at the heart of the saint in ecstasy.

115

Opposite S. Maria della Vittoria, at the corner of Via XX Settembre, is the *Church of S. Susanna,* appointed for the worship of American Catholics. Rebuilt by Maderna in 1603, its interior is richly decorated with frescoes illustrating the history of the two Susannas, that of the Old Testament (Apocrypha) and the Susanna who suffered martyrdom under Diocletian. Opposite this church, in the background of the piazza, the Church of S. Bernardo, built into a round, domed corner hall of the Baths of Diocletian (p. 136).

Proceeding westward from S. Bernardo on Via XX Settembre and past the Quattro Fontane, S. Carlo, and S. Andrea al Quirinale (p. 73), we reach the *Piazza del Quirinale,* a new marvel of Roman architecture, in which site, monuments, and palaces unite into an admirable whole. The piazza is dominated by the mighty group of colossal statues of the Horse-tamers Castor and Pollux. The statues come from the Baths of Constantine, the ruins of which lie under the Palazzo Rospigliosi. The inscriptions on the pedestals, with the names of Phidias and Praxiteles, were designed to protect the statues from destruction by Christian zealots. The obelisk comes from the Mausoleum of Augustus, the basin of the fountain from the Roman Forum. The fountain dates from 1818.

The *Palazzo del Quirinale* was begun in 1574 as a summer residence for the Popes in the gardens of the Cardinal Ippolito d'Este, the builder of the Villa d'Este in Tivoli (p. 174); with its numerous additions, it was completed only in the 18th century. Pius IX was the last Pope to bless the people from its loggia; it is now the residence of the president of the Italian Republic.

To the right is the Palazzo della Consulta, with an excellent Rococo façade, built by Fuga in 1739; it is now the Italian Colonial Office. Further down, next to it, the Palazzo Rospigliosi, built in 1603 over the ruins of the Baths of Constantine. Later it came into the possession of Cardinal Mazarin, the great minister of Louis XIV of France, and was enlarged by Maderna.

We descend the staircase at the Piazza del Quirinale, go

down Via della Dataria, turn right at the corner, and after a few steps find ourselves before the *Fontana di Trevi,* perhaps the most beautiful fountain in the world. The spring which feeds the aqueduct is said to have been revealed by a maiden to Roman soldiers perishing of thirst, and is therefore called Acqua Virgo. It is brought from the Campagna, a distance of 12 miles, and was first used in 19 B.C. by Agrippa for his baths. The richly figured façade, in front of the Palazzo Poli, was executed by Salvi in 1762 after Bernini's design; in the center, the sea-god Neptune in a shell-chariot drawn by tritons. An amiable superstition bids the departing traveler throw a copper coin over his shoulder into the basin, with head averted, to ensure his return to Rome.

Opposite the Fontana di Trevi is the Church of SS. Vincenzo ed Anastasio. We pass this and proceed through the Via S. Vincenzo and Via Lucchesi to the Piazza Pilotta. At the left is the modern building of the Università Gregoriana, directed by Jesuits. Opposite it is the Istituto Biblico.

A few steps along its right side take us to the elongated *Piazza SS. Apostoli,* with the *Church of the SS. Apostoli* at its left. It was founded in the 4th century, rebuilt in the Baroque style by Fontana in 1702. In the porch, to the right, a relief with oak wreath and eagle, excellent work of the period of Emperor Trajan. In the spacious interior, at the end of the left aisle, over the entrance to the sacristy, is the tomb of Clement XIV by Canova. The painting of the martyrdom of the Apostles Philip and James by Muratori on the principal altar is reckoned the greatest of its kind in Rome.

Opposite the church is Bernini's façade of the Palazzo Odescalchi. Next to the church is the extensive site of the Palazzo Colonna, the origins of which date back to Pope Martin V.

The Piazza SS. Apostoli opens on the short Via Cesare Battisti, which leads to the *Piazza Venezia.* The piazza is named after the impressive *Palazzo Venezia,* the construction of which was begun by the Venetian Pope Paul

S. MARIA IN ARACOELI

II in the mid-15th century with stones from the Colosseum. In 1560 Pius IV donated it to the Republic of Venice, and it became the residence of the Venetian envoy and, from 1797-1916, of the Austro-Hungarian ambassador to the Holy See. The interior has a magnificent but unfinished court. The museum of the palace makes accessible splendid rooms with excellently restored frescoes of the early Renaissance and rich collections.

At the south side of the Palazzo Venezia is the entrance to the *Church of S. Marco,* restored in Baroque style in the 18th century. The 9th-century mosaics of the apse show Christ between saints, who (on the left) escort the founder of the church, Pope Gregory IV. In the corner of the piazza are remains of a colossal statue of Isis, from the temple of the Egyptian deities nearby. The statue is popularly called Madama Lucrezia, after a famous courtesan of the Renaissance.

The Piazza Venezia is dominated by the colossal marble

CAMPIDOGLIO

mass of the National Monument to King Victor Emmanuel II (1885-1911), the founder of the united Kingdom of Italy. At the center, the equestrian statue of the King, and behind it the tomb of the unknown soldier.

In front, to the left of the left-hand fountain, remains of the tomb of C. Publicius Bibulus, from the end of the Roman Republic.

A few steps along the Via del Mare, at the right of the National Monument, take us to the Piazza Aracoeli and to the wide staircase leading to the Piazza del Campidoglio.

The *Church of S. Maria in Aracoeli* stands on the spot where, according to Medieval legend, the Tiburtine Sibyl announced to Emperor Augustus the birth of Christ. In Roman times the temple of Juno Moneta and the offices of the Roman mint occupied the site. It is the Roman church richest in Medieval memories. The lofty stairway, dating from 1348, is the only public construction carried out by the Romans during the Popes' exile at Avignon. The interior of the church has twenty-two ancient columns. The naval symbols on the ceiling recall the victory

119

over the Turks at Lepanto in 1571. In the first chapel to the right of the right aisle are beautiful frescoes of Pinturicchio, with scenes from the life of St. Bernardino of Siena (*c*. 1485). The two pulpits at the end of the nave are the work of the Cosmati, *c*. 1200. At the right wall of the right transept is the tomb of Pope Honorius IV. At the wall of the left transept, a statue of Leo X. A chapel near the sacristy is devoted to the worship of the Bambino Santissimo, and contains an image of the Christ Child richly ornamented with jewels. Formerly it possessed its own golden carriage, in which to visit the sick. Between the second and third chapels of the left aisle is a statue of Paul III.

The *Campidoglio* (the square of the Capitol) is reached by the wide and gradually ascending stairs designed by Michelangelo. To the left a shady walk, to the right the carriage road. In the park at the left is a small bronze memorial (1887) to Cola di Rienzi, the illusionist Tribune of the People; after a brief rule over Rome he was murdered in 1354 and his body burned.

The Campidoglio owes its present aspect to Michelangelo's design of 1538, and it is the perfect square. At the balustrade in front stand the two groups of the Dioscuri (Castor and Pollux) with their horses. Next are the so-called Trophies of Marius, probably monuments of Domitian's war against the Germans. Next, to the left, the statue of Constantine the Great; to the right, that of his son Constantine II. The square is dominated by the magnificent equestrian statue of Marcus Aurelius, originally gilded, brought here from the Lateran by Michelangelo. The Emperor, on his heavy horse of northern breed, appears in all simplicity as the dispenser of peace. On the left, the *Capitoline Museum*, built under Innocent X in the 17th century; for its collections of antiquities see p. 142. On the right is the *Palazzo dei Conservatori*, rebuilt in 1564-1568 by Michelangelo's pupils according to his plans; its museums are treated on p. 146. In the center of the square is the *Palazzo del Senatore*, built over the ancient Tabularium (p. 14); the façade was executed in

TEMPIO DI FORTUNA VIRILIS

1592 by Rainaldi after the plans of Michelangelo. To the sides of the stairway ancient figures of river-gods, Tiber on the right and Nile on the left; in the center a fountain, above which is a seated statue of Roma. The *Tabularium* may be reached by the steep stairs between the Palazzo dei Conservatori and the Palazzo del Senatore. It contains splendid architrave fragments from the temples of Concordia and of Vespasian in the Forum Romanum, and the recently discovered Chapel of Veioris with the headless statue of that ancient Roman deity.

A stair at the right of the Palazzo del Senatore leads to the Via Tempio di Giove, and down this street is the Belvedere Tarpeo, with its excellent view of Forum and Palatine. From here we descend to the Piazza della Consolazione, and then through the Via S. Giovanni Decollato to the *Piazza Bocca della Verità*.

In the left background of this piazza, near the small Church of S. Giorgio in Velabro, is the *Arcus Argen-*

tariorum, erected 204 A.D. in honor of Emperor Septimius Severus, his wife Julia Domna, and his sons Geta and Caracalla, by the guild of money-changers and bankers. Next to it, the *Janus Quadrifrons,* probably a triumphal arch of the age of Constantine. Opposite this and near the Tiber is the small *Temple of Fortuna Virilis,* which was called S. Maria Egiziaca when it served as a church. It possesses a porch and decorative Ionic half-columns. It dates from the first half of the 1st century B.C., and perhaps belonged to Portunus, the god of the Tiber harbor nearby. The other graceful structure at this picturesque site is the round so-called *Tempio di Vesta.* It dates from the end of the Republic or the beginning of the Empire. Its present appearance dates back to a Medieval restoration. The beautiful *Triton Fountain* dates from 1715. Opposite is the *Church of S. Maria in Cosmedin,* also called Bocca della Verità ("the mouth of truth"). According to popular legend, the triton mask at the left of the vestibule holds fast any liar who thrusts his hand into its mouth. The 8th-century church was admirably restored in the late 19th century. The beautiful Campanile dates from the 12th century. The simple interior contains eighteen ancient columns, a mosaic pavement, pulpits, Easter candelabra, and an 11th-century episcopal chair.

We return through the Via del Mare, and find on our left, before the large modern administration building of the municipality of Rome, the Casa di Crescenzio, a Medieval private house decorated with numerous fragments from late antiquity.

Next to the modern administration building, on the left, the *Church of S. Nicola in Carcere,* with ancient columns in its left exterior wall and in its three-aisled interior. These come from Roman temples of the Forum Holitorium, or vegetable market, which occupied the site. To this Forum also belong the recently excavated remains of halls on the opposite side.

Further to the left is the *Theater of Marcellus.* As in the Colosseum, an Ionic order is superimposed on a Doric.

TRITON FOUNTAIN AND TEMPIO DI VESTA

The stage extended along the Tiber side. The theater accommodated fourteen thousand spectators. It was begun by Julius Caesar, completed by Augustus in 13 A.D., and dedicated to the memory of his nephew Marcellus. The three elegant Corinthian columns with architrave and frieze, adjoining to the right, belong to the Temple of Apollo which the Consul C. Sosianus restored in 32 B.C.

Behind the Theater of Marcellus, the Via Portico d'Ottavia leads past the *Church of S. Angelo in Pescheria*. The Corinthian columns with architrave and attic of its portal and the columns of its façade are remains of the temple precinct which Augustus built in 27 B.C. and dedicated in the name of his sister Octavia. The extant remains are from the restoration effected by Septimius Severus and Caracalla in 205 A.D.

The continuation of the Via Portico d'Ottavia opens on the broad Via Arenula. We follow this to the right, and soon come to the square before the Teatro Argentina (on the left). At a level lower than the street are the remains

THEATER OF MARCELLUS

of *Four Temples* of the late Republic in a row, one round and three rectangular. We do not know to what deities these temples were dedicated.

We return by Via Arenula to the Piazza Benedetto Cairoli, on the right. From this, to the right, Via de' Giubbonari leads past the Church of S. Carlo ai Catinari to the *Campo dei Fiori*, the popular fruit and flower market, where once heretics and witches were burned. As the pantheistic philosopher Giordano Bruno was burned here on February 17, 1600, his statue, erected in 1887, stands at the center of the square.

From the Campo dei Fiori three short streets, running toward the Tiber, lead to the Piazza Farnese, which is dominated by the mighty structure of the *Palazzo Farnese*, the most magnificent in Rome. It was begun before 1514 by the then Cardinal Alexander Farnese, later Pope Paul III. Its architect was Antonio da San Gallo the Younger,

PIAZZA NAVONA

and its stones came from the Colosseum and the Theater of Marcellus; the cornice and parts of the grandiose courts are Michelangelo's (after 1546).

We return to the Campo dei Fiori and thence by the Via dei Baullari to the Corso Vittorio Emanuele. To our right is the *Palazzo Massimi alle Colonne,* the residence of one of the oldest noble families of Rome. It was built, with its compact colonnaded courts, by Baldassare Peruzzi (died 1536). In its rear chambers two German printers printed the first books in Rome, in 1467. To our left is the gracefully small *Palazzo Linotte,* called Farnesina dei Baullari, built about 1523. The Museo Barracco p. 130), rich in Greek originals, has recently been removed to this building.

Behind it and to the left, the simple and noble *Palazzo della Cancelleria* rises from the *Piazza della Cancelleria.* This building was originally the seat of the administration of the Papal States. It is the most significant structure of the early Renaissance in Rome. The rhythmic articulation of the façade is executed in three orders—Doric, Ionic, and Corinthian. It was built with blocks from the Colosseum on the design of the great architect and theoretician Leon Battista Alberti of Florence. Inside, a noble arcaded court.

Next to the Palazzo Massimi alle Colonne is the small *Piazza S. Pantaleone* with the monument of the Italian statesman Marco Minghetti. Behind it, the Palazzo Braschi (1780), the last of the mansions built by a Pope for his family. At its rear is the so-called Pasquino, on which anonymous satirical epigrams used to be affixed—whence the term pasquinade. The Pasquino is the fragment of a Roman copy of a Greek marble group of the 3rd century B.C., showing Menelaus as he carries the body of Patroclus from the battlefield. The fragment was much studied by Renaissance sculptors.

The majestic *Piazza Navona,* the fifth of the incomparable squares of Rome, opens to our view a few steps to the right of the Pasquino. On the left is Rainaldi's Palazzo Doria-Pamphili (1644-1648), and next to it the Church of S. Agnese (p. 78). In form the piazza coincides with the stadium which Emperor Domitian built for athletic contests in 80 A.D.; remains of the stadium were uncovered when new streets were opened up to the north and east. But what gives the piazza its vitality are the three fountains. The so-called "Moro" with a triton, to the south, is by Bernini. The central fountain, also by Bernini, represents the four continents by figures of the Danube, Ganges, Nile, and Rio della Plata. The Nile is said to be covering his eyes in order to escape the sight of the façade of S. Agnese, which was the work of Borromini, Bernini's rival for papal favor. Domitian's obelisk comes from the Circus of Maxentius on the Via Appia. The third fountain shows Neptune with nereids and sea-horses; though executed in 1878, it blends admirably into the square.

ROME'S MUSEUMS OF ANTIQUITIES

MUSEO NAZIONALE ROMANO O DELLE TERME
MUSEO CAPITOLINO
MUSEO DEL PALAZZO DEI CONSERVATORI
MUSEO DEL LATERANO
MUSEO NAZIONALE DI VILLA GIULIA
MUSEO E GALLERIA BORGHESE

INTRODUCTION

THE museums of Rome possess the greatest assemblage of Greco-Roman art to be found anywhere in the world. But without some preparatory study the modern visitor is apt to be helpless before their exhibits, and for several reasons.

In the first place, there is the superabundance of plastic works. Furthermore, following the usage of centuries, which has extended almost to the present, many of the exhibits have been "restored" or reworked. Statues were seldom recovered in a state sufficiently complete and undamaged to satisfy the decorative requirements of past centuries, when complete and finished works were sought. Hence statues received new arms and legs, or heads that did not belong to them, and heads received new ears and noses. To present the illusion of a carefully finished whole, the old marble was worked over. Hence the numerous "restored" statues in the older Roman museums, particularly the Vatican (p. 56) and Capitoline (p. 142), which repel the spectator by their chilly smoothness. Special knowledge and practice are required to see through the modern disguises and perceive the genuine originals.

Plastic art is alien to most moderns. Painting engages more immediate sympathy by the charm of its colors and the interest of its subject. In modern life plastic art is encountered chiefly in public monuments of famous men. In most cases they are falsely conceived or displayed, or the work of bad or mediocre artists. Sculpture has little claim on general interest.

But in the Greco-Roman world the reverse was true. Pediment figures and metopes in Greek temples, votive offerings to the deity in the round or in relief, figures of victors in the public athletic contests, honorific statues of statesmen and thinkers, grave monuments, gave sculpture a patent religious and political importance difficult for us to imagine. We know the names of hundreds of Greek sculptors of whom no work has survived. The smallest Greek town had its artists and an abundance of plastic art. The only comparable phenomena are the plastic riches of Romanesque and Gothic cathedrals or the delight in pictorial representation characteristic of the Renaissance and the Baroque.

But for appreciation of the Roman museums another factor must be kept in mind. Most of the exhibits of Greek character are Roman copies. Only Greek science, Greek philosophy, Greek techniques could transform the sober Roman peasants, merchants, and soldiers into the civilized rulers of the world. Roman contact with the Greek cities of the south came early. Greek religious ideas were soon adopted. The Etruscans, whose influence upon Rome was early and deep, were themselves saturated with Greek influence. Finally, with the conquest of Greece and the Greek East in the 2nd century B.C., Greek art made its way into Rome in a continuous and irresistible stream, and became part of the general culture. Ownership of a unique Greek masterpiece that had been brought to Rome might be coveted by many; or a Roman might wish to deposit in his own temple the duplicate of some Greek masterpiece which could not be removed from its Greek shrine. These appetites—some religious, some ethical, some aesthetic—gave rise to the practice, unparalleled in later

SPINARIO, CONSERVATORI

ages, of wholesale copying of works of a bygone age. Workmanlike copies of Greek masterpieces were produced for Roman amateurs, sometimes in a dozen examples. The preferred medium of the Greek sculptor was not painted marble but bronze, and the chances of bronze surviving historical vicissitudes are slight. The Roman copyist translated bronze originals into marble, and hence we have Roman copies of many works of which the Greek originals have perished. Such, for example, are the excellent copy of the Aristogiton from the Tyrannicide group in the new Muso dei Conservatori (p. 149); the Marsyas of the Myron group in the Lateran (p. 151); the Doryphorus of Polycitus in the Braccio Nuovo of the Vatican (p. 59); the Apollo Belvedere (p. 58); the Apoxyomenus of Lysippus (p. 58); the portrait of Demosthenes (p. 59). There are bad Roman copies, but there are also excellent ones, as for example the Youth from Subiaco (p. 140) and the Venus from Cyrene (p. 140) in the Museo delle Terme.

But the museums of Rome also possess a number of magnificent Greek originals. With one, the Funeral Stele of the Youth, in the Vatican (p. 57), we have already become acquainted. The Museo dei Conservatori has a small hall devoted mainly to Greek originals (p. 148). The crowning glory of Greek art in Rome is the so-called Ludovisi Throne in the Museo delle Terme (p. 138), which is unequaled even in Athens. Another Greek original of the first rank is the Dying Niobid in the same museum (p. 140). The Museo Barracco is especially rich in smaller Greek originals and fragments (p. 125).

Besides the factor of original or copy, the modern observer will do well to bear in mind another consideration that will increase his appreciation of ancient art. Modern art, aside from church art, which, for the time being, plays a minor role in it, serves the aesthetic requirement of decoration for homes or public buildings and squares. Ancient Greek art was in the first instance and with but few exceptions religious. It served as decoration for the temple or as votive offering to the deity. Its content is determined by religious myth. Its point of departure is neither imitation of nature nor any of the merely aesthetic objectives characteristic of modern art, but the obligation to serve the deity or the religious ideas connected with the deity with the most beautiful object within man's reach. The most beautiful and most precious object within the reach of ancient man was man himself. The climax of Greek art is therefore the representation of the human figure, whether in an image of the god conceived in human form or in a votive offering dedicated to the god. All that the human figure implies as vital force, as natural organic growth, as articulated harmony, as image of human destiny, is given purest expression in three-dimensional sculpture. Hence the plastic human figure dominates ancient art as it has never done in any subsequent period.

Greek plastic art of the type called *archaic* (9th to 6th centuries B.C.) must be studied in the museums of Greece;

LAOKOON, VATICAN MUSEUM

Rome has only the She-wolf of the Conservatori (p. 147) of that period. The vase collections of the Vatican (p. 60) and the Villa Giulia (p. 155), however, are rich in monuments of archaic painting, but time can scarcely be found for them in a brief tour. About 480 B.C. archaic art gives way to the *severe* style, the greatest monument of which are the pediment sculptures of the temple of Zeus at Olympia, of about 460 B.C. Rome's finest example of this style is the so-called Ludovisi Throne (p. 138) in the Museo delle Terme. The Aristogiton in the Tyrannicide group (p. 149), the charming figure of the Boy Extracting the Thorn (p. 147), and other works in Room VIII of the new Museo dei Conservatori, belong to this style. Its special attraction lies in the struggle between a delicate timidity of form, and restraint in feeling on the one hand, and new breadth and strength in conceptions of nature and humanity on the other.

The *great classical* style uses the achievements of the preceding epoch with freedom and power. Its greatest monument is the Parthenon and its sculptures in Athens (448-432 B.C.), but its effects endured until late in the 4th century B.C. Its great masters are Phidias and his pupils Alcamenes and Agoracritus; Myron, creator of the Discus Thrower in the Terme (p. 139) and the Marsyas in the Lateran (p. 151); Polyclitus of Argos, creator of the Doryphorus in the Vatican (p. 59); and many others. The classical style achieves the complete mobility and freedom of the human figure. It develops a new three-dimensional representation of material substance, operating from specific axes of the perpendicular and the horizontal. It creates new and spacious images of the gods, stately and sublime. To it belong the dignified temple figures of Hera and Demeter in the Rotonda of the Vatican (p. 57), the Artemis from Ariccia (p. 137), the Apollo from the Tiber (p. 140) and the Niobid (p. 140) in the Terme, the Demeter in the Salone of the Capitoline Museum (p. 145), the Athena in the Museo Nuovo (p. 149), and the Relief of the Peliads in the Lateran (p. 151).

The *art of the 4th century* B.C. is also classic. Its great masters are Praxiteles and Cephisodotus, Scopas, Timotheus, Leochares, and finally Lysippus; and these have many others in their train. Fourth-century art marks no sudden break, but rather a gradual development of 5th-century art in new realms of representation, in a new accentuation of the spiritual, in a new delicacy in the corporeal. Praxiteles' Youth Watching a Lizard (p. 57) and his Aphrodite of Cnidos (p. 58) we have already encountered in the Vatican. A kindred piece is the Leaning Satyr in the Capitoline (p. 145). The tender and dignified god in the Sala della Biga of the Vatican (p. 62) may belong to Cephisodotus. The enthroned god in Room VI of the Terme (p. 137) doubtless echoes a large statue by Bryaxis. The Apollo Belvedere in the Vatican (p. 58) is conjectured to be a work of Leochares. The Leda of the Capitoline

AUGUSTUS FROM PRIMA PORTA, VATICAN MUSEUM

(p. 144) is referred to Timotheus. The Capitoline Aphrodite (p. 144) is a development from Praxiteles'. The ideal in portraiture of the decade 340-330 B.C. is represented by the Sophocles in the Lateran (p. 151). The aspirations of the century culminated in the powerful personality of Lysippus, the contemporary of Alexander the Great. Among his works are the Apoxyomenus in the Vatican (p. 58), the Silenus with the infant Dionysus in the Braccio Nuovo (p. 59), and perhaps also the Seated Ares in the Ludovisi collection of the Terme (p. 138).

Hellenistic art embraces the centuries between Alexander (died 323 B.C.) and the inception of an indigenous Roman art in the 1st century B.C. It is distinguished by a new realism in regard to nature, enhanced pathos in representing human emotions, boldness in depicting movement, and extreme technical virtuosity. The principal seats of Hellenistic art were Pergamum, Rhodes, and Alexandria. Pergamene art is represented by the large group of the Gaul and his Wife in the Ludovisi collection of the Terme (p. 138) and the Dying Gaul of the Capitoline (p. 146). The splendid Head of a Satyr in the Conservatori (p. 148) dates from the 2nd century B.C. A typical portrait of the beginning of the 3rd century B.C. is that of Demosthenes in the Vatican (p. 59); the differences from the type represented by the Sophocles of the Lateran (p. 151) are patent. Among the choice works of the Hellenistic age are the Maid of Anzio (p. 140), the Youth of Subiaco (p. 140), the Sleeping Hermaphrodite (p. 140), the Aphrodite of Cyrene (p. 140)—all in the Terme. To the waning Hellenistic period belong the Laocoon in the Vatican (p. 58), the bronze Boxer (p. 141), and the so-called Hellenistic Ruler (p. 141) in the Terme.

The *art of the Roman Republic* created a new realism in its portraiture. Excellent examples are the double bust in the Sala dei Busti of the Vatican (p. 57) and the funeral relief of a husband and wife in the Museo Nuovo (p. 149).

The development of the *art of the Roman Empire* is apparent in its great monuments: the Ara Pacis Augustae (p. 107), the Columns of Trajan (p. 30) and of Marcus Aurelius (p. 110), the reliefs on the Arches of Titus (p. 36), Septimius Severus (p. 17), and Constantine (p. 35). The history of Roman portraiture under the Empire may be illustrated by the likenesses of almost every Emperor and his family, chiefly in the collections of the Stanza degli Imperatori of the Capitoline (p. 144) and Room VIII of the Terme (p. 141). The series begins with the statues of Augustus from Primaporta (in the Vatican: p. 59), and from Via Labiacana (p. 142), and the colossal so-called Juno Ludovisi (p. 138), and ends with the colossal Constantine in the Conservatori court (p. 146) and the bronze portrait of his son Constantine II in the Sala dei Bronzi of the Conservatori (p. 150).

Sarcophagi constitute an important item in the art of the Empire. Their reliefs are either of a mythological-

MUSEO DELLE TERME, CLOISTER

religious character and reproduce creations of Greek art,
like the numerous specimens in the entrance halls of the
Terme (p. 136), or they depict the grim character of Roman military command, like the great Germani Sarcophagus in the Terme (p. 137) or the Ludovisi sarcophagus
with battle scenes (p. 139). Christian art took over the
form and pictorial arrangement of the sarcophagus and
filled it with a new content. Good examples are the Junius
Bassus sarcophagus in the Grottoes of the Vatican (p. 45)
and numerous specimens in the Terme (p. 136) and the
Museo Cristiano of the Lateran (p. 152).

For travelers pressed for time, visits to the museums of
the Terme and of the Palazzo dei Conservatori are to be
recommended; these two museums contain the best recent finds, and without restorations—which is not the
case in the older collections of the Vatican and the Capitoline Museum.

MUSEO NAZIONALE ROMANO O DELLE TERME

The gigantic complex of the Baths of Diocletian and his co-ruler Maximilian was dedicated in 305-306 A.D. It extends from the round building at the beginning of Via G. Amendola, from which the tram for Albano and Frascati (p. 168, 170) leaves, to the Church of S. Bernardo. The curve of the Piazza d'Esedra reproduces the semicircular apse of its outer wall. The arrangement was similar to that of the Baths of Caracalla (p. 93). Three thousand bathers could be accommodated simultaneously, and the Baths also provided for sports, lectures, and all kinds of entertainment.

The main hall of the bath proper was transformed by Michelangelo into the *Church of S. Maria degli Angeli* in 1561. The entrance is opposite the Piazza d'Esedra. At the right of the round vestibule is the tomb of the painter Maratta (died 1713), and at the left that of the painter Salvator Rosa (died 1673). At the right of the corridor to the main hall is the magnificent statue of St. Bruno by Houdon. According to Michelangelo's plan, the great hall of the bath—298 by 89 ft. and 92 ft. high—would have remained a unified interior, with its entrance at the short end on the right; this design is spoiled by the present entrance and the removal of the principal altar to the center. Part of the gigantic red granite columns come from the bath. Inlaid in the pavement at the right is a meridian with signs of the zodiac. At the right, near the principal altar, is the monument of Marshal Armando Diaz, leader of the Italian army in World War I. The paintings on the walls are largely from St. Peter's. Among them, at the left of the nave, is the Mass of St. Basilius before Emperor Valens, by Subleyras; at the right, St. Jerome among the Hermits by Girolamo Muziano; the landscape is by the Fleming Paul Bril.

The *Museo delle Terme* is entered through the court at the right of the church. In the magnificent entrance hall of the museum, originally vaulted, against the wall op-

LUDOVISIAN THRONE, MUSEO DELLE TERME

posite the entrance, is No. 80941, a colossal statue of
Artemis from Ariccia, a Roman copy of a Greek temple
statue of the mid-5th century B.C. On the entrance wall
opposite, No. 112327, a Roman sarcophagus decorated
with battle scenes with over 100 figures: A Roman general
(face unfinished) in battle against Germans; at either side
of the battle, a pair of excellently conceived Germans
beneath a trophy. On the wall at the left of the entrance,
No. 112444, a sarcophagus showing the enthusiastic hunts-
man Hippolytus, scorning the love of Phaedra.

Room II is on the left. At the left wall are splendid
architectural fragments from Emperor Aurelian's great
Temple to the Sun (3rd century A.D.).

Room III, to the rear, contains Christian sarcophagi.
We return to the main hall, and thence, left, to the adjoining Room VI. On the left, the portal of the Temple
of Augustus at Ankara in Asia Minor is reproduced in
plaster; No. 108361, in the portal, is a pleasing statue
of an enthroned god, a Roman copy of a Greek original
of the middle of the 4th century B.C., perhaps by Bryaxis.

We return to the main hall, thence to the court, with
numerous sculptural fragments, and then to the right into

the vaulted room with two semicircular apses, adjoining which is a long room containing Roman mosaics of various date, some very handsome. From the apsidal hall we reach the garden, enclosed by the Great Cloister, built in 1565 from Michelangelo's design, with an abundance of funeral monuments and statues. From the garden we pass to the museum proper, through a vestibule, and enter the small cloister at the left which contains the *Ludovisi Collection*. Immediately to the right, on the entrance wall, is No. 8598, a colossal head of a goddess, a Greek original of about 480 B.C. In the small holes locks of hair and gold ornaments were affixed. No. 8624 represents Hermes as the clever and amiable god of persuasion; this is a Roman copy of a Greek work of the mid-5th century B.C. At the corner is the colossal group of the Gaul who, in despair at being conquered, has slain his wife, and is thrusting his sword into his own breast; this is a Roman copy of a monument commemorating the victory of a Pergamene king over the Gauls (beginning of the 2nd century B.C.). Immediately to the right is the entrance to a small chamber which contains the so-called Ludovisi Throne (No. 8570), the chief jewel of the museum. The monument is surely not a throne, but part of a larger work (other parts are in the Boston Museum of Fine Arts) of religious significance. The principal face represents not that of Aphrodite rising from the sea, as is often stated, but the ascent of a goddess from the underworld, supported by two Horae, into the realm of light. The left face presents a nude female flautist, the right a veiled woman offering incense. The monument is a Greek original of the most refined workmanship, dating from about 460 B.C. No. 8631, at the rear wall, is the colossal head of the famous Ludovisi Juno (1st century A.D.), probably a portrait of the Elder Agrippina, mother of Emperor Caligula, who was deified after her death. The third work in this room is the Sleeping Medusa, a Hellenistic work.

Returning to the cloister, we find the Ludovisi Ares (No. 8602) at our right: The god of war is anxiously inspecting a battlefield. This is a Roman copy of a work

LUDOVISIAN JUNO, MUSEO DELLE TERME

of the second half of the 4th century B.C., perhaps by Lysippus. No. 8569 at the end of the next wall is the great Ludovisi sarcophagus with battle scenes, showing a Roman general in the midst of battle against Gauls (mid-3rd century A.D.).

We leave the Ludovisi collection and proceed to the rooms on the opposite side which contain the principal works in the museum. Room I contains three major works: No. 56039, an athlete throwing the discus; this is a Roman copy of a masterpiece of Myron, of the middle of the 5th century B.C. No. 1053, a youthful athlete with the olive branch of victory in his hair. The green basalt of the Roman copy is intended to represent the bronze of the original, by a follower of Polyclitus (second half of the

5th century B.C.). No. 72274, Niobid from the Gardens of Sallust. Struck between the shoulders by Artemis' arrow, the innocent daughter of Niobe is shown looking pitifully to heaven as she sinks to the ground. This is a fine Greek original of about 440 B.C. from a temple pediment, from which two figures in the Glyptothek Ny Carlsberg in Copenhagen also derive.

Room II: No. 608, the Apollo from the Tiber, and hence slightly weatherbeaten. The long-haired god gazes benevolently upon the viewer. This is a Roman copy of an exquisite Attic work of between 450 and 440 B.C. No. 10614, a magnificent torso, is a Roman copy of Polyclitus' Heracles, of about 430 B.C.

Room III: No. 1075, at the center, is the Youth of Subiaco, running to catch a ball. This is a beautifully patinated Roman copy of a Hellenistic bronze of the 3rd century B.C. At the left of the entrance is No. 51, Juno from the Palatine, a Roman copy of a stately cult statue by a follower of Phidias of about 430-420 B.C. At the left is No. 1085, an austere head of Hygeia, the Greek goddess of health; this is an excellent Roman copy of a work of Scopas (mid-4th century B.C.). No. 622, Dionysus from Tivoli with a panther skin, is a Hadrianic adaptation of a work from the 4th century B.C.

Room IV: No. 50170 is the famous Maid of Anzio. Her left hand holds sacrificial implements; she is probably a servant of Iphigenia, taken from a group. This is an excellent Roman copy of a Hellenistic original of the 3rd century B.C. No. 124679, Head of Apollo from Butrinto, repeats the head on the statue of Apollo from Anzio, No. 121302; this is a Roman copy of a Greek work of the end of the 4th century B.C. No. 1087, in the middle of the room, is the Sleeping Hermaphrodite, a Roman copy of a Hellenistic work of the 3rd century B.C. No. 603, Head of a Dying Persian, is a Roman copy of a work of the Pergamene school of the 2nd century B.C.

Room V: No. 72115, opposite the entrance, is the Venus of Cyrene, an excellent Roman copy of a Hellenistic work of the 2nd century B.C. No. 1049 at its left is the mag-

NIOBID, MUSEO DELLE TERME

nificent bronze statue of the so-called Hellenistic Ruler, a Greek original of the 1st century B.C. Next to it, No. 1055, the brutal figure of a seated boxer. The inscription on the fiststrap identifies the artist as the Apollonius who fashioned the torso in the Belvedere of the Vatican (p. 58).

Room VI contains unimportant Roman works of colored marble.

We return to the entrance hall with the sales counter for photographs and catalogues. Opposite it is Room VII, which contains bronzes taken from the ships salvaged from Lake Nemi and supposed to have belonged to Caligula. Excellent heads of a Medusa, a wolf, and a leopard (1st century A.D.).

Room VIII, adjoining, contains a fine collection of Roman portraits, of which we list a few. No. 1043, a charmingly fresh head of a girl, dating between 30 and

40 A.D. No. 618, Emperor Nero. No. 124129, an excellent portrait of the Younger Agrippina, mother of Nero, dating before 59 A.D. No. 56230, excellent togaed statue of Augustus from the Via Labicana. No. 58561, the youthful Lucius Verus. No. 639, bust of a Chief Vestal, of the 3rd century A.D., from the House of the Vestals in the Forum (p. 24). No. 124486, outstanding portrait of the mid-3rd century A.D. No. 330, Emperor Vespasian. No. 124491, Emperor Hadrian. No. 644, Emperor Gallienus.

MUSEO CAPITOLINO
(p. 142)

Here too we can notice only a few principal works.

In the beautiful architectonic ensemble of the court, rising above the fountain, is the so-called Marforio, a colossal statue of a benign river-god, reclining in serene tranquillity. This is a Roman work of the 1st century A.D.

Passing through the corridor to the right, we enter, opposite the stairway, first the fifth room and then the sixth. Here on the right (No. 5) is a large sarcophagus depicting a battle between Greeks and Gauls; this is a Roman work of the late 2nd century A.D., following Hellenistic Greek motifs. In the seventh room is a large sarcophagus of the beginning of the 3rd century A.D., with recumbent figures of husband and wife, and portraits. The front panel shows the youthful Achilles being discovered by Odysseus and Diomedes on the Island of Scyros, where he had been concealed among the daughters of Lycomedes to keep him from the dangers of the Trojan War. The short left end shows Achilles' farewell to Lycomedes; the right end, Achilles arming himself for battle. The rear panel shows the venerable Priam kneeling before Achilles in petition for the body of his son Hector whom Achilles had slain.

We return to the stairs and ascend to the upper floor. In the corridor at the left, near the window, a Roman sarcophagus of the first half of the 2nd century A.D.; its relief of a battle of Greeks and Amazons follows Hellenistic patterns. At the right of the corridor is the *Dove*

MAID OF ANZIO, MUSEO DELLE TERME

Room, so called from the excellent mosaic on the right wall
showing doves perched on the rim of a metal basin filled
with water; this is a Roman copy of a Hellenistic Pergamene original. Beneath is a child's sarcophagus of the
middle of the 3rd century A.D.; its relief shows Prometheus
creating mankind and Athene infusing men with life.
Numerous Roman portraits, some very fine. At the center

of the short wall, above, a Roman sarcophagus relief shows
Dionysus returning in triumph from India in a chariot
drawn by panthers, a theme suggested by Alexander the
Great's expedition to India in 328 B.C. At the first window
on the left is the so-called Tabula Iliaca, a marble relief
with miniature scenes from the Trojan War.

We return to the corridor. No. 49, at the left, colossal
head of a goddess, a Greek original of the early 3rd century; the empty eye-sockets once held eyes. Down the
corridor and to the right is No. 20, Fleeing Psyche
crouched before Cupid's arrow; this is a Roman copy of
an early Hellenistic work of about 300 B.C. To the right is
the *Gabinetto della Venere,* with the Capitoline Venus
(No. 1) in its niche. This is a Roman copy, preserved
intact, of a Greek variant of Praxiteles' Aphrodite of
Cnidos, dating from the end of the 4th century B.C. No. 2,
Leda is embraced by Zeus in form of a swan. Roman
copy of a Greek original by Timotheus. First quarter of
the 4th century B.C. In the corridor at the right No. 29, a
solemn and stately statue of Athene; this is a Roman copy
of a Greek work of the beginning of the 4th century B.C.

From the corridor we turn right to the *Stanza degli
Imperatori* with numerous portraits of Roman Emperors
and their kin. At the window on the right is an excellent
portrait of a Flavian lady of about 90 A.D. At the window
overlooking the Campidoglio, a portrait of the Elder
Drusus, brother of Emperor Tiberius, wearing the oak
crown; its date is *c.* 9 B.C. Above, at the left, No. 2, an excellent portrait of the youthful Augustus, full of nervous
tension (*c.* 38 B.C.).

The adjoining *Stanza dei Filosofi* contains a collection
of portraits, some significant, of Greek and Roman poets
and thinkers. Nos. 4 and 5 above, Socrates. Nos. 44 and
45 below, Homer. No. 64, Epicurus. No. 75, Cicero. No.
88 is an excellent character study of an unknown figure
of the beginning of the 3rd century B.C.

The *Salone* (large hall): In the center, two centaurs of
gray-black marble, by Aristeas and Papias (2nd century
A.D.). Cupids were mounted upon the centaurs' backs;

DOVE BASIN, MUSEO DELLE TERME

the youthful centaur answers the rein cheerfully, the bearded one is recalcitrant. At the right of the door at the long wall is No. 20, Apollo, copied from a famous Greek work of 470-460 B.C.; the forearms and thighs are modern. No. 24, Roman copy of a Greek temple goddess, of the school of Phidias (430-420 B.C.). At the windowed wall, No. 33, Wounded Amazon, a Roman copy of one of the four Amazon figures by four contemporaries of Phidias, which stood in the sanctuary of Artemis at Ephesus; the right arm, the left forearm, and the hand with drapery are restored; c. 440 B.C.

The *Stanza del Fauno Rosso* is named for the red marble satyr of the Hadrianic period at its center. At the center of the short wall, a Roman sarcophagus (No. 3) of the second half of the 2nd century A.D., with the story of the love of Selene, the lunar goddess, for the shepherd Endymion. On the right, Selene approaches her sleeping love; on the left, she has to leave him at dawn. The lid does not belong to this sarcophagus. To the right, a child's sarcophagus showing the nurture of the new-born god

Dionysus; this is a Roman work of the beginning of the 2nd century A.D., in imitation of Greek models of the early 3rd century B.C.

The *Stanza del Gladiatore* is named after the Dying Gaul (No. 1) at its center, wrongly thought to be a gladiator. This is a Roman copy of a figure on a monument commemorating the victory of King Attalus I of Pergamum over the Gauls. No. 4, at the left, is another Roman copy from the series of Amazons mentioned above; the head does not belong to this statue, and the right arm is restored. To the right is a fine head of Helios (No. 3), copied from a Hellenistic work of the 3rd century B.C.; bronze rays were fitted into the holes in the hair-fillet. The magnificent head of Dionysus opposite (No. 5) is the Roman copy of a Hellenistic work of the early 3rd century B.C. Near the exit, handsome statue of a goddess (No. 2), Pergamene work of the first half of the 3rd century B.C.; the arms are new.

PALAZZO DEI CONSERVATORI—MUSEO NUOVO

In the courtyard of the Palazzo dei Conservatori, at the right, are the head—7½ ft. high—and limbs of the colossal statue of Constantine the Great, from the Basilica of Constantine in the Roman Forum (p. 32). On the left are reliefs representing Roman provinces, and weapons from the Temple of the deified Hadrian.

Ascending the staircase, at the first landing we see reliefs showing Emperor Marcus Aurelius sacrificing at the Temple of Jupiter Capitolinus; riding in his triumphal chariot; receiving subject barbarians. The fourth relief at the left, with restored head of Marcus Aurelius, represents Emperor Hadrian's arrival in Rome and his reception by the goddess Roma.

At the left of the corridor, the statue of Charles I of Anjou, King of Naples and Sicily, who ordered Conradin von Hohenstaufen beheaded in 1268.

The large hall at the right of the corridor has frescoes by the Cavaliere d'Arpino, depicting the battle of the

DYING GAUL, MUSEO DELLE TERME

Horatii and Curiatii and other legends from the early history of Rome. The room contains a marble statue of **Pope Urban VIII** by Bernini, and a bronze statue of **Pope Innocent X** by Algardi.

Through Room II, *dei Capitani,* we reach the corner room (*dei Trionfi*). At its center is the famous bronze Spinario, a boy extracting a thorn from his left foot; this is a Roman copy of a Greek work of about 460 B.C. Room IV, *dei Fasti:* At its center, the Capitoline She-wolf, an archaic Greek bronze of about 500 B.C. The hind legs were damaged by lightning in 65 B.C.; the Romulus and Remus underneath are additions of the early Renaissance.

We return to the corridor through the adjoining rooms, then turn right to the long gallery. We pass through Room I (*dei Fasti Moderni*) to Room II (*dei Fasti Moderni*), and find, to the left, a Roman sarcophagus of the 2nd century B.C., showing Dionysus in a chariot drawn by centaurs, with a train of satyrs and maenads; the relief bears many traces of the original painting.

Stairs from the right of the gallery lead to the *Galleria Orti Lamiani.* At its center, the Esquiline Venus, a nude in the act of tying her hair; this is a Roman copy of a Greek work of about 450 B.C. The handsome head of a Silenus on the right (No. 92) is a Roman copy of a Pergamene work of the first half of the 2nd century B.C. No. 8 on the right is a portrait of Emperor Commodus, who is represented as Hercules.

A small stair leads down to the *Sala dei Magistrati;* by the window on the left is an excellent portrait from the 3rd century A.D.

We cross the corner room to the *Sala delle Opere Arcaiche.* No. 12 at the center is not a charioteer but rather a boxer; it is a copy of a Greek work of about 460 B.C. At the wall on the left is the handsome funeral stele of the Girl with the Dove (No. 9), a Greek original of about 480 B.C. At the center of the main wall is the headless statue of a swooping Victory, a Greek original of 470-460 B.C. At the right wall is an excellent lion's head (No. 2), a Greek original of about 480 B.C.

We return to the gallery, and thence to the garden at its right. Built into the wall are portions of the large city plan of Rome which Emperor Septimius Severus put up near the Forum. No. 54 at the left is a charming statue of Antinoüs, Emperor Hadrian's favorite, with panther skin and pine wreath. Immediately adjacent are two copies of the same Greek figure, found in the same house—Cupid with a goose, looking up wistfully. The Greek original belonged to the beginning of the 3rd century B.C.

The gallery ends at the wall of the Temple of Jupiter Capitolinus, which was first dedicated in 509 B.C. At the right, the base of a statue of Cornelia, mother of Tiberius and Gaius Gracchus (*d.* 133-121 B.C.), the ill-starred advocates of social reform in the Roman Republic.

We descend a few steps to the right and pass through Rooms I, II, and III of the Museo Nuovo into Room IV. At the entrance (No. 15) is the charming group of a satyr embracing a maenad, a Roman copy of a Hellenistic original of the 2nd century B.C. At the center, a Muse leaning upon a rock, an attractive Roman copy of a Hellenistic work of the end of the 2nd century B.C. Above, at the left, handsome colossal head of Heracles (No. 21), perhaps a Greek original of about 100 B.C. Beneath it, splendid torso of a reclining Hercules, Roman copy of a Greek original of the mid-4th century B.C.

Room V: The magnificent Athene in the corner (No. 15) is a Roman copy of a temple statue by Cephisodon of Athens, of the first half of the 4th century B.C. No. 57, opposite, is a portrait of the great Athenian tragedian Sophocles, a Roman copy of an early work of the 4th century B.C. No. 6 is a replica of the Aphrodite of Arles in the Louvre, a Roman copy of a Greek work of the mid-4th century B.C.

Room VIII, adjoining to the right, contains the principal works of the museum and, in the center, remains of the Temple of Jupiter Capitolinus. At the right, a statue of Aristogiton, the elder of the two friends who attempted to liberate Athens from its tyrants in 514 B.C. This is an excellent Roman copy of the work of Critius and Nesiotes of 477 B.C. In the right corner, magnificent portrait (Roman copy) of an Athenian general of the end of the 5th century. At the left, statue of a discus-thrower at the moment of casting; Roman copy, possibly of a work by Naucydus of the end of the 5th century B.C. Adjoining, No. 47, magnificent statue of a goddess, probably Core, the younger of the goddesses of the Eleusinian Mysteries; this is a Roman copy of an Attic work of about 340 B.C. In the niche, colossal statue of Athene, Roman copy, probably of a work by Cresilas of about 430 B.C. At the right wall, splendid female statue with a head of Athene that does not belong to it; Roman copy of a statue by Phidias of about 440 B.C.

Room VI adjoins. No. 6, on the left, funeral relief of a husband and wife from the Republican period, mid-1st century B.C.

Room VII: A Roman funeral monument with four busts in niches, from the end of the Republican period. At its left, excellent bust of the Augustan period, recently conjectured to represent the Roman poet Horace. No. 9, on the wall at the right, is a fragment of an excellent relief showing the façade of an Ionic temple with an Amazon battle in the pediment; this is a Roman work of the Augustan period. In the corner, portrait of Emperor Domitian. At the entrance wall, the handsome prow of a ship ending in a boar's head, once part of a fountain decoration, perhaps from the Golden House of Nero (p. 34). At its left, excellent portrait of the mid-3rd century A.D. At the right, portrait of Emperor Pupienus.

We return to follow along the wall of the Capitoline Temple to the *Sala Republicana*. At the center, relief of the horseman Marcus Curtius who leaped into the chasm of Lacus Curtius in the Forum (p. 22). At the left, statue of a togaed man, carrying the busts of two ancestors, from the first half of the 1st century A.D. On the right, statue in peperino: Orpheus playing the lyre. This is one of the few monuments of early Roman art of the 2nd century B.C. The statue is probably from a tomb, the figure of Orpheus representing the Orphic belief in immortality.

We return to the gallery, and thence to the *Sala Orti Mezenaziani,* first on the right. No. 16 on the left, magnificent attacking boxer; Roman copy of a work by a contemporary of Lysippus, about 330 B.C. No. 1094, at the wall on the right, is a handsome relief of a maenad with sword and fawn; a Roman Neo-Attic copy of a Greek original of the end of the 5th century B.C. No. 7 is an excellent copy of the head of an Amazon, which belongs to the statue in the Salone of the Museo Capitolino (p. 145).

In the adjoining *Sala dei Bronzi,* at the left, colossal portrait of Emperor Constantine II.

We pass through the *Sala Castellani,* with its fine *Collection of Greek vases,* into the *Sala della Lettica.* Here is a bronze chariot with mountings, depicting scenes from the life of Achilles, 3rd century A.D.

The next room at the right contains a large sarcophagus, with recumbent figures of husband and wife, their faces unfinished, and figures of Meleager and Atalanta hunting the Calydonian boar (beginning of the 3rd century A.D.).

ROMAN SHE-WOLF, PALAZZO DEI CONSERVATORI

MUSEO DEL LATERANO

The entrance is in the Palace of the Lateran, near the main façade of S. Giovanni in Laterano (p. 65).

Room VI: No. 350, colossal seated statue of Emperor Tiberius with oak wreath. No. 351, the Younger Agrippina, wife of Emperor Claudius and mother of Nero. No. 352, colossal statue of Emperor Claudius with oak wreath. No. 365, colossal head of Emperor Augustus.

Room VII: No. 379, the Marsyas of Myron, a Roman copy of the bronze original of 450-440 B.C. Marsyas recoils before Athene, who has thrown the flute at his feet. No. 382, handsome portrait statue of the tragedian Sophocles, Roman copy of a Greek work of about 330 B.C. No. 388, relief of Medea and the daughters of Pelias, who, upon her advice, are prepared to slay their father and boil his dismembered limbs in a cauldron to restore him to youth; this is a Roman copy of a Greek work of about 430 B.C.

Room VIII: Nos. 390 and 427, monuments of the tomb

of the Haterii from Centocelle, with excellent portraits of the deceased; Flavian work of about 90 A.D. No. 429, jamb, with delicately designed roses.

Room IX: On the floor, excellent mosaic of Heraclitus: Nile landscape, theater masks, remains of a meal swept on the dining-room floor—oysters, crabs, snails, a mouse nibbling nuts, grapes, and the like, an imitation of the mosaic by Sosus of Pergamum, the "unswept dining room" (2nd century A.D.).

Room X: No. 661, colossal Poseidon, with right foot on the prow of a ship—a Roman copy of a Greek work of about 300 B.C.

Room XI: No. 682, Roman sarcophagus of the end of the 2nd century A.D. The myth of Phaedra and Hippolytus, after Greek models: Phaedra, wife of Theseus, confesses her love for her stepson to her nurse; Hippolytus rejects her advances and is killed in a boar hunt.

Room XV: No. 914, niche containing a mosaic of the Roman forest-deity Silvanus, of the 2nd century A.D.

Room XVI: 954, remains of a funeral fresco: Orpheus, Eurydice, Pluto, and Proserpina, deities of the underworld, and Ocnus tirelessly braiding a cable, which an ass behind him steadily devours. At the left is the gate of Hades, with Cerberus and the gatekeeper.

MUSEO CRISTIANO DEL LATERANO

The *Galleria dei Sarcofaghi* on the ground floor at the left of the entrance contains Christian sarcophagi. No. 111, Crossing of the Red Sea, 4th century A.D. No. 104, reliefs in two rows (first half of the 4th century A.D.). In the upper row, from left to right: the Holy Trinity creating man; Adam and Eve being assigned the earth; the tree of knowledge and the serpent; busts of the deceased; the miracle at the marriage at Cana; the miracle of the loaves and the fishes; the raising of Lazarus. The lower row contains: the Magi before Mary and the infant Jesus; the healing of the blind man; Daniel in the lions' den; Habakkuk offering him a loaf; Peter's denial and the cock; the

VILLA GIULIA

arrest of Peter; Moses striking the rock. No. 103, statue of Christ as the Good Shepherd. No. 174, a columned sarcophagus of the mid-4th century A.D. From left to right: Abraham sacrificing Isaac; Moses with the scroll of the Law; Paul adoring the Lord; Christ enthroned over heaven; Peter receiving the New Testament; Christ before Pilate, who is washing his right hand.

MUSEO NAZIONALE DI VILLA GIULIA IN VIALE DELLE BELLE ARTI

The Villa of Pope Julius III was built as the summer residence and bathing place for the Pope by Vignola, Pirro Ligorio, Ammanati and others, and is a prime example of the mannered Italian style. With its accessory buildings, vineyards, and pergolas, it originally extended down to the Tiber, and the Pope could reach it from the Vatican by boat. As a museum it contains rich collections from excavations in the vicinity of Rome, principally of Etruscan art and Greek vases.

Immediately upon entering we obtain a perspective of the elaborate architectural arrangement, with the nymphaeum (fountain room) in the background. Directly on the left is the Antiquarium with numerous Etruscan mirrors of engraved bronze, showing Greek influence, weapons, vessels, and the like. Isolated on the left, the Chigi wine jug of the early archaic period of Greek figure painting (7th century B.C.) decorated with numerous delicate miniature-like figures—warriors setting forth, a lion hunt, a judgment of Paris.

The semicircle of the porticus has delightful ceiling decorations of children and satyrs in apertures of the vine arbor. Here, a stairway on the left leads to the second story, containing finds from Falerii and its environs, the territory extending from the right bank of the Tiber. The case at the center of Room III has excellent Greek vases: at the center, a large drinking bowl with dancing maidens, of about 460 B.C., and, to its right, a handsome bowl of about 420 B.C. showing Heracles' introduction to Olympus.

We return to the porticus, and turn the corner on the left to reach the rooms containing the finds from Veii. In the large room, the over life-size terra-cotta figure of the Apollo of Veii, from a group which crowned the roof-ridge of a temple. Apollo was shown contesting possession of the hind with Heracles (see the adjacent fragment); the head of Hermes on the wall at the right belonged to the same group as did also the headless female figure with infant over the right breast, and the handsome torso at the left. The group is our most important example of archaic Etruscan art of about 480 B.C. On the wall at the right are excellent revetment tiles with Medusa heads.

To the right, into the long room. Here, at the end, the limestone figure of the Warrior from Capestrano in the province of Aquila, a quite unique representative of archaic Illyrian art of the 6th century B.C. This is the tomb figure of a king, with face-mask, wide-brimmed hat, and weapons.

We return to the garden, and, through the door at the left rear, visit the *Augusto Castellani Collection*. In the center of Room XXI, a reconstructed archaic Etruscan battle chariot of bronze. The adjoining rooms contain a collection of Greek and Etruscan vases.

We return to the entrance of the museum, and thence to Room I on the right, which contains finds from Palestrina—bronzes, weapons, vessels, ivories. In an alcove beyond the left exit of this room, the so-called Ficoroni Cista, a round bronze container with richly figured engraved designs: the Argonauts on their way to Colchis; Pollux vanquishing Amycus, king of the Bebrycians, in boxing. The work is by the Roman Novios Plautios, after a famous Greek painting of the 4th century B.C.

The right-hand portion of the semicircle gives access to the rooms containing finds from Cerveteri, Civita Castellana, Segni, Conca, and Satricum. Room VI has an excellent Etruscan terra-cotta sarcophagus with recumbent figures of husband and wife (*c.* 500 B.C.).

The rooms following house a rich collection of architectural terra cottas, Greek vases, votive terra cottas, and the like. In Room VII (*Civita Castellana*), in the last case at the center, an outstanding portrait in painted terra cotta of the 1st century B.C. In Room VIII, on the right, at the end, is an excellent terra-cotta Apollo, from a temple pediment in Civita Castellana. Over it, a fine terra-cotta Hermes. Both date from the end of the 4th century B.C.

In the garden, to the rear, on the right, is a reconstruction of the Etruscan Temple of Alatri (4th century B.C.).

VILLA BORGHESE (VILLA UMBERTO I)—MUSEO E GALLERIA BORGHESE

The inaccessible Villa Doria Pamphili (p. 84), the Villa Medici (p. 113), and the Villa Borghese are the only approximately completely preserved specimens of the Roman "villa," with its shady walks, terraced gardens, fountains, and the like, created by great architects as summer residences for the Roman nobility of the 17th and 18th centuries. Until well into the 19th century numerous such villas were to be found on the periphery of the city.

The *Villa Borghese* was built for Scipione Borghese, nephew of Pope Paul V, in the early decades of the 17th century, and furnished with rich collections of art; later it was much enlarged and altered. In 1902 it was purchased by the Italian government, combined with the valuable Borghese collection of paintings, the most important in Rome (previously housed in the Palazzo Borghese), and connected with the park on the Pincio by a bridge.

The principal entrance is by the Neo-Classic portal built by Canina in 1835, at the right of the Porta del Popolo. There are other entrances opposite the Porta Pinciana, and near the Giardino Zoologico between Via Aldovrandi and Via Mercadante.

The main entrance leads through a shady lane of evergreens to a crossing at the Fontana di Esculapio with its ancient statue; the left path leads to the separate Giardino del Lago, with an artificial lake and an imitation antique Tempio di Esculapio. Leaving the Giardino del Lago on the opposite side, we reach, at the right of the main road, the Piazza di Siena, surrounded by handsome old stone pines; here much frequented international equestrian games take place each spring. The main road ends at the modern ruins of the Neo-Classic Tempio di Faustina. Here we turn right into the carriage road and come to the pretty Fontana dei Cavalli Marini by Unterberger (1791).

A few steps farther a path to the left leads directly to the *Casino Borghese*. This was built by the Dutch Jan van Santen (Giovanni Vasanzio) in 1613-1616. The museum contains sculpture ancient and modern, including the principal works of Bernini, and painting, including principal works of the masters of the Venetian school and of Raphael. Here only the most important works are mentioned.

Groundfloor, vestibule: In the right half, at the left, a large battle sarcophagus of the age of Septimius Severus (193-211), of the same order as that in the Terme (p. 137).

156

GIARDINO DEL LAGO

Great entrance hall: The ceiling fresco by the Sicilian
Mariano Rossi (1774) shows Marcus Furius Camillus
breaking off negotiations with the Gallic King Brennus,
who conquered Rome in 390 B.C. In the pavement, a
fragment of a large mosaic showing gladiatorial combats,
from Torrenova; this is post-Constantinian work, of the
4th century A.D. In the left niche, a fine Hellenistic torso,
restored as a dancing satyr. At the long wall (XLI), the
third statue from the left is a fine togaed portrait of
Augustus. At the right short wall, to the left, colossal
portrait of Emperor Hadrian, and to the right, one of
Emperor Antoninus Pius. We move right, to

Room I: At the center, the smoothly chill statue of Paolina Borghese, sister of Napoleon, represented as a reclining Venus, by Canova (1809). The model for a statue
of John the Baptist, at the entrance wall, is an early work
of Houdon.

Room II: At the center, David with his sling, an early
work of Bernini (1619). At the right and left are sar-

cophagi of the 3rd century A.D., illustrating the labors of Hercules.

Room III: At the center, Daphne fleeing Apollo's love is transformed to a laurel tree; this is a masterpiece of the young Bernini (1616).

Room IV: At the center, Pluto abducting Proserpina, by Bernini. The porphyry busts of Roman Emperors are 17th-century works. The niches at the long wall contain Roman copies of fine Greek originals of the 4th and 3rd centuries B.C.

Room V contains a good replica of the Sleeping Hermaphrodite, after a Greek work of the 3rd century B.C.

Room VI: At the center, Aeneas, bearing his father Anchises from fallen Troy. This is perhaps a work of Pietro Bernini, father of Lorenzo. At the right wall a statue of Truth, by Bernini (1645). The altarpiece, a Risen Christ with saints, is by Girolamo da Cremona, and comes from Viterbo Cathedral (1470).

We retrace our steps, ascend the spiral stairs beyond Room IV to the second floor, and enter Room VIII. On the left, Fra Angelico da Fiesole's Last Judgment. Above it (No. 343), Adoration of the Infant Jesus, by the Florentine Piero di Cosimo. At the window wall (No. 371), Raphael, unfinished portrait of a woman with a unicorn (1506). The so-called Fornarina (576), attributed to Raphael, can hardly be entirely from his hand. No. 397, portrait of a man, is an early work of Raphael (c. 1502), under the influence of Perugino. No. 4 is an excellent Madonna by the Florentine Filippo Lippi (1437). No. 369, on the main wall, Raphael's Entombment of Christ, painted in 1507, at the beginning of his monumental style. No. 348, opposite the windows, Madonna with St. John and angels, by the Florentine Sandro Botticelli. No. 433, Madonna with St. John, by the Florentine Lorenzo di Credi.

Room IX is largely devoted to the Venetian school. On the main wall at the left, No. 185, Lorenzo Lotto's portrait of a man in black (c. 1530). Adjacent, No. 396, portrait of a man by Antonello da Messina. No. 21, portrait of a

PAOLINA BORGHESE, MUSEO BORGHESE

German by Bartolomeo Veneto, a 16th century work. No. 176, Madonna with the Infant Jesus, illustrates the mature style of Giovanni Bellini. At the window, Antonello da Messina's saint in a blue veil. On the other main wall, No. 326, Venus and Cupid with a honeycomb, by Lucas Cranach the Younger. No. 547, the Archangel Raphael and Tobias, by Savoldo da Brescia. At the left near the exit, delicate work of Lorenzo Lotto in old frame: Madonna surrounded by Sts. Jerome, George, Sebastian, John the Baptist, Anthony, and Catherine (1524).

We retrace our steps and turn right into Room X, devoted to Florentines of the High Renaissance. At the middle of the left wall, No. 334, Andrea del Sarto's Madonna and Child and John the Baptist. Adjacent, at the right, No. 408, Francesco Salviati's excellent portrait of Pope Marcellus II as Cardinal (c. 1548). No. 577, opposite, Andrea del Sarto's Holy Family.

Rooms XI and XII have less important pictures.

Room XIII has the principal works of Caravaggio, the revolutionary naturalist of Baroque painting. No. 110, on the entrance wall, Madonna and the Infant Jesus with the serpent (c. 1605). At its left, near the window, No.

455, David with the head of Goliath. The unnumbered picture ascribed to Caravaggio shows Narcissus admiring the reflection of his beauty in the water. Nos. 534 and 136, Roman boys with fruit, by Caravaggio. No. 53, on the short wall, Diana hunting, by Domenichino of Bologna, a smooth, cold painting. The John the Baptist at its right (No. 267) is ascribed to Caravaggio. Nos. 265 and 266 on the main wall opposite the windows, magnificent portraits of Cardinal Scipione Borghese, the founder of the Villa Borghese, by Bernini (1625). At the center of the room, Bernini's terra-cotta model for the equestrian statue of Louis XIV of France (c. 1670). The black marble statue of Sleep (No. 100) is by Algardi.

Room XIV: The Entombment on the entrance wall (No. 411) is an early work (c. 1605) of Peter Paul Rubens. No. 554, at the window, self-portrait by Bernini (c. 1629). No. 555, splendid portrait of a boy by Bernini. Opposite the Rubens, No. 376, Andrea Sacchi's fine portrait of Monsignor Clemente Merlini. No. 545 at its right is a second self-portrait of Bernini. Straight ahead to

Room XV: No. 26 at the left, and No. 649 at the center of the left wall, are Adorations of the Shepherds by Jacopo da Ponte da Bassano. At the right and left of the latter, sketches for large paintings by El Greco (Domenico Theotocopuli of Crete), the great mystic of Baroque painting—Adoration of the Shepherds with the Ascension of Christ, and Baptism of Christ with a manifestation of the Holy Trinity; about 1510. No. 38, opposite, the adulteress before Christ, a delightful early work of Tintoretto.

Room XVI has less important paintings.

Room XVII has Flemish and Dutch works. No. 572, the Concert, excellent painting by Hendrick For ter Bruggen (1629).

We turn back and to the right into Room XVIII. At the left of the entrance wall, No. 217, the sorceress Circe, painted by Dosso Dossi of Ferrara for the castle of Duke Alfonso I d'Este in Ferrara. No. 125, opposite, Jupiter transformed into a shower of gold visits Danae; in the splendor of its silvery tone, one of the greatest works of Correggio of Parma.

Room XIX contains the Venetian gems of the collection. No. 157, at the left of the entrance wall, Madonna and Child, and Sts. Barbara and Justina, is ascribed to Palma Vecchio. No. 163, in the corner, is Palma Vecchio's Madonna and Child as half-figures with Sts. Jerome and Anthony. No. 147, at the center of the left wall, is the so-called Sacred and Profane Love by Titian, a masterpiece of the great painter's early period. No. 188 is Titian's St. Vincent Ferrer. No. 170, on the right wall, Venus binding Cupid's eyes while nymphs fetch his bow and arrows, is a work of Titian's maturity, painted *c.* 1565. No. 137 at the center, John the Baptist preaching, with Christ appearing in the distance, is an early masterpiece of Paolo Veronese. No. 101, next to it, is Veronese's St. Anthony preaching to the fish of the sea. No. 194 in the corner, Christ scourged at the pillar, is a late work of Titian.

EXCURSIONS IN THE VICINITY OF ROME

THE EXCAVATIONS AT OSTIA

T HE station of the Rome-Ostia-Lido electric railway is in front of the Porta S. Paolo (p. 87). We descend at the *Ostia Scavi* station. At the right is the mid-15th century castle built by Julius II while he was Cardinal. The straight road at the left leads to the excavations.

Ostia signifies mouth or exit, and is the spot where the Tiber originally emptied into the sea. The city was established in the second half of the 4th century B.C. as a fortress to control the mouth of the Tiber, and was settled by a Roman colony. In the Republic and early Empire its importance as a naval station and as a harbor for provisioning Rome steadily increased, until the gradual silting of the harbor and retreat of the sea forced Emperor Trajan to construct the new harbor of Porto north of Ostia in 103 A.D. But life continued in Ostia, until the invasions of the barbarians and malaria put an end to it in the 5th century. After earlier plundering excavations, the systematic uncovering of the city began in 1909 and has given us a picture of an ancient mercantile town which is in a certain sense a pendant to Pompeii. About two thirds of the city area have been excavated, and the mounds in the stretches of sand toward the sea indicate clearly where significant ruins still remain underground.

On the right is the *Museum,* with an abundance of significant finds, of which only a few can be listed here.

OSTIA. THEATER

Entrance hall: No. 2 is the right half of a sarcophagus of the 2nd century A.D. with scenes from the story of the youthful Achilles among the daughters of Lycomedes. No. 5 is a funeral relief showing a Roman husband and wife clasping hands (2nd century A.D.).

Room I contains portraits of Roman Emperors and their kin. No. 17, a colossal Trajan, is one of the best existing portraits of that Emperor. No. 18 is a head of Augustus. No. 19 is a head of the youthful Domitian. No. 21 is a portrait statue of Julia Domna, wife of Septimius Severus, as the goddess Ceres. No. 20 shows Emperor Trajan in armor. No. 24 is a portrait statue of Sabina, wife of Emperor Hadrian, as Venus, after a famous work by a follower of Phidias. No. 25 shows Sabina as Ceres. No. 28 is a very handsome portrait of the Elder Faustina, wife of Antoninus Pius. No. 29 is a bust of Septimius Severus in armor. No. 32 is a colossal head of Hadrian. No. 34 is a very fine child's sarcophagus, showing young children who, in imitation of their elders, play on musical instruments at a banquet, and wrestle in a gymnasium; this is a Greek work of the 2nd century B.C.

Room II contains portraits. No. 38 is an excellently preserved portrait of C. Volcacius Myropnous, Antonine work of the second half of the 2nd century A.D. No. 42, colossal portrait of a man, is an outstanding monument of the end of ancient sculpture and the transition to Medieval; it dates from the 5th century A.D. No. 45, portrait of a man, is an excellent example of the post-Constantinian style at the end of the 4th century A.D. No. 55 is a late togaed statue of the beginning of the 5th century A.D. No. 56, a marble shield with an excellent portrait of the age of Trajan. No. 61 represents Julia Procula as the goddess Hygeia, after a famous Greek work of the mid-4th century B.C. No. 67, portrait of an old man, dates from the end of the Republic.

Room III contains Greek works. No. 85 is an excellent Roman copy of a Greek portrait of the great Athenian statesman Themistocles (*c.* 470 B.C.). No. 98 is a Roman copy of a 3rd century B.C. Greek portrait of a philosopher, perhaps Hippocrates of Cos, the founder of scientific medicine. No. 109 is a fine head of Eros, with eyes of glass; the Greek model of this work belongs to the mid-5th century B.C. The splendid colossal torso of Zeus (No. 114) is an excellent Roman copy of a Greek work of the mid-4th century B.C. The handsome statue of Apollo leaning against a laurel trunk (No. 117) is a Roman copy of an Attic work of the middle of the 5th century B.C. No. 121 is a majestic headless statue of a god with his left foot stepping on a stone, bearing the inscription of its donor, C. Cartilius Poplicola. This is an excellent Roman copy of a Greek work of the school of Lysippus, of the 4th century B.C.

Room IV contains less important reliefs, frescoes, and mosaics.

Room V contains monuments pertaining to the history

OSTIA. HOUSE OF THE MILLS

of religion. The large group of Mithras slaying the bull
(No. 149) was copied by the Athenian sculptor Critius
from a Hellenistic work of the 3rd century B.C. The fine
funeral slab of a boy holding a pet bird in his left hand
and an olive branch in his right (No. 150) dates from the
early 4th century A.D. No. 157, relief of the haruspex
(inspector of sacrificial entrails for divination), D. Fulvius
Salvis, is our sole existing monument of Republican art of
the first half of the 1st century B.C. The relief shows a
statue of Hercules being fished out of the sea, and the
lots of Hercules being consulted. No. 158 is a sarcophagus
lid with the recumbent figure of the chief priest of Cybele
whose cult was brought from Asia Minor; this dates from
the end of the 3rd century A.D. No. 159, from the same
tomb, in the Isola Sacra, shows the same priest with two
torches before an altar with spruce and a small figure of
the god Attis. In No. 160 the same priest offers sacrifice
before a cult image of Cybele.

Room VI has plans of the excavations of Ostia, and also smaller remains.

The *Excavations* are entered from the left of the Museum by Via delle Tombe, which was used for burials immediately outside the city gate, and is lined with remains of sarcophagi and funeral monuments. A few steps take us to the principal gate, which is fortified by two square towers; here the lower strata of the wall of the original Republican castrum (fortress) have been laid bare. On the left of the Piazzale della Vittoria is a colossal statue of Minerva Victoria with Corinthian helmet and shield; the missing left hand probably held out a wreath. The statue dates from the end of the 1st century A.D. Proceeding along the *Decumanus* (main thoroughfare) we come to the *Via dei Vigili* on the right. On the left side of this street are large Baths with a gymnasium. The main hall has a large mosaic in white and black, showing the sea with tritons, nereids, and dolphins. The ancient stairs lead to a terrace which commands a wide view. Behind the Baths is the building of the military city police; about 200 A.D. these numbered some 600 men.

We return to the Decumanus. At the corner of the Via delle Corporazioni, on the left, is the *ancient theater,* which has been restored for modern performances. Its final enlargement was under Septimius Severus and Caracalla. Its stage is 125 ft. wide. The Piazzale delle Corporazioni—the Square of the Corporations—behind the stage was a center of shipping agents, with sixty-three offices. At the center of the square is a small temple of the patron deity of the whole. The offices of the individual firms are fitted with mosaics showing likenesses of ships and the names of the proprietors. Next to the theater, four small temples of unknown deities stand on a single podium. In the block following, behind a row of retail shops fronting on the street, is one of the great grain warehouses characteristic of Ostia—sixty-four storage rooms grouped about a rectangular court. At the rear of the next block of buildings on *Via dei Molini* rooms with mills for grinding grain were connected with bakery shops. Next to this rear por-

OSTIA. TEMPLE OF THE CAPITOLINE GODS

tion is the *Casa di Diana*, so named for a terra-cotta relief of the goddess of the hunt in its court. Water pipes in the house, rooms decorated with frescoes, mosaic floors, balconies giving a view of the street, stairs preserved up to the third story, suggest that this house was one of the most modern of ancient Ostia. Adjoining is the *Casa dei Dipinti*, with good frescoes, some well preserved. We return to the Decumanus, and so reach the *Forum*. At the right, on a lofty podium with a monumental stairway, ruins of the *Temple of the three gods of the Capitol*, Jupiter, Juno, Minerva—which belonged in every Roman community. Opposite are the ruins of a Temple of Rome and Augustus. At the west side was a basilica, similar in plan to the Basilica Julia in the Roman Forum (p. 15). Behind the basilica is a square with a round temple of the 3rd century A.D., similar to the Pantheon (p. 76); this is the last monumental temple in the city. To the northwest is the *Via degli Horrea Epagathiana et Epaphroditiana.* The granaries (horrea) for which the street is named are identified by their nominal adjectives in the owners' inscriptions over the monumental gate. The great granaries are grouped about an arcaded court, as in a Renaissance palazzo. Nearby is a private house with its first floor preserved; its terrace affords a fine panorama. Next are the most recently excavated Baths; here there is a large round, domed hall, with magnificent mosaics in the vaulting. In an adjoining room is a latrine with frescoes of four of the seven sages of Greece on its walls. The Latin sayings refer to the good offices of the room.

From the Ostia Scavi station the railway goes on to the *Ostia Lido,* with its much frequented beach, and then to the *Castel Fusano* station, with its fine pine forest.

THE ALBAN HILLS
FRASCATI AND GROTTAFERRATA

Railway from the Stazione Termine, tram (tram station in the Via Regina Giovanna di Bulgaria, near Stazione Termine), and road pass to the left of the huge arches of the aqueduct which Emperor Claudius completed in 49 A.D. On the right are the tombs and cypresses of the Via Appia. Farther to the right are the ruins of a large villa of the late Empire, called Sette Bassi.

The town of *Frascati,* which suffered severely in World War II, is famous for its wine and for the splendid villas of the Roman nobility, with their parks and fountains. The most regal of these is the Villa Aldobrandini, before the entrance to the city, built by Giacomo della Porta in 1598-1605 for Cardinal Aldobrandini, nephew of Pope Clement VIII.

At the Piazza del Gesù in the city is the Church del Gesù, which has a handsome ceiling fresco of architectural painting in perspective by the Jesuit Father, Pozzo.

From Corso d'Italia, past Via Massai, then, left, Via alla Villa Lancellotti, lead to a path which ascends between walls to a fine Baroque gate, through which a large old

CASTEL GANDOLFO. PAPAL PALACE

oak has forced its way, and then to the entrance to the Villa Falconieri, built by Borromini in 1648. This has a magnificent terrace and a unique pond surrounded by cypresses.

From the Piazza Garibaldi the Via delle Fratte leads to a square, at the right of which, near the great portal of the Villa Borghese-Parisi, is the entrance to the Villa Mondragone. This was built under Gregory XIII, in part by Vignola. The fountain and the ornamental sprays are by Fontana. The majestic terrace gives a magnificent view of the Roman Campagna.

The sight in the wine center *Grottaferrata*, between Frascati and Marino, is the *Abbey* of Greek Basilian monks, a few steps to the right of the tram station of the Corso Vittorio Emanuele line. The Abbey was founded in 1004 by Emperor Otto III, and was made into a fortress in 1484 by Julius II before he became Pope. Of the old church only the vestibule with its carved wooden portal of the 11th century is preserved. Above it is a mosaic of Christ, Mary, and St. Basil. The Campanile is of the 11th century. The walls of the interior have fresco remains of the 13th century, and, on the triumphal arch, a mosaic of the 13th century, the Twelve Apostles at Pentecost. The right aisle gives access to the Chapel of St. Nilus with charming frescoes by Domenichino (1610). The principal scene, on the left wall, shows Emperor Otto III visiting St. Nilus; the squire in green, holding the Emperor's horse, is a self-portrait of Domenichino. Opposite the altar is a baptismal font of the 11th century. The Monastery Museum has an excellent funeral relief of a seated young man, a Greek original of the end of the 5th century B.C.

From Grottaferrata a cable car ascends to *Rocca di Papa*, a picturesque eyrie, about 2200 ft. above sea level. An hour's climb takes us to the summit of Monte Cavo, (3115 ft. above sea level). Here was the shrine of Jupiter Latiarius, the sanctuary of the allied Latin cities, which was older than Rome itself. There are no remains of a temple, but there are traces of the ancient road leading up to it.

CASTEL GANDOLFO—ALBANO—LAGO DI ALBANO ARICCIA—LAGO DI NEMI

The Lago di Albano, partially surrounded by forests, is a volcanic crater lake, 6 miles in circuit, 560 ft. maximum depth. On its steep bank is *Castel Gandolfo*, on the site of the Latin Alba Longa, the mother-city of ancient Rome. At the Piazza del Plebiscito is the fortress-like papal palace, built by Urban VIII in the first half of the 17th century. Turning left at the southeast end of Via Garibaldi, we reach the *Villa Barberini*, the present summer residence of the Popes. This villa was built over a villa of Emperor Domitian. The Galleria di Sopra, with its handsome evergreens and fine view of the lake, takes us past the villa and to Albano in some thirty-five minutes.

From Castel Gandolfo the road through the Galleria di Sotto leads to *Albano*, 1260 ft. above sea level, which lies

LAGO DI NEMI

over the site of military barracks built by Septimius Severus in 195 A.D. for the Second Parthian Legion. At the right of the main street, Larga Mazzini, is the entrance to the Villa Communale, a pretty park of pines with a splendid view. Via Aurelio Saffi on the left leads to the proximity of the round Church of S. Maria della Rotonda, built on the site of a fountain of Emperor Domitian. At the left, behind the high-perched Capuchin Church, the Galleria di Sopra from Castel Gandolfo joins the road. From here a pretty forest path circles the lake to the west to the former monastery of Palazzuola, in the garden of which the rock tomb of a Roman consul is preserved.

The main road through Albano passes an ancient monument on the right called the Tomb of the Horatii and the Curiatii. This is a large rectangular base, once surmounted by five blunt cones (of which two remain); it can hardly have been a tomb. Beyond this a viaduct, 194 ft. high, takes us to *Ariccia*. To the left of the entrance, beyond the viaduct, is the *Palazzo Chigi* with a fine park; a tip to the gate-keeper will gain admittance. Opposite is the handsome round Church of S. Maria dell'Assunzione, by Bernini (1664).

Immediately to the right of the Palazzo Chigi a road running first along the park wall and then through a chestnut grove ascends, in about two hours, to Rocca di Papa (p. 170) and beyond to Monte Cavo (p. 170), or it circles the Alban Lake to Marino and thence to Grottaferrata (p. 169).

From Albano, the tram reaches the wine center Genzano, three miles away. From the left of the Piazza Dante Alighieri in Genzano the Via Garibaldi and then a road to the right lead down to the *Lago di Nemi*. This dark crater lake is 3½ miles in circuit, with a maximum depth of 110 ft. Its name is derived from the Latin *nemus*, grove, because the present gardens, through which the road runs, were the site of the shrine of Diana Nemorensis, the great sanctuary of the Latin League. The village of Nemi and its castle of the Ruspoli family afford fine views of the calm lake.

ACQUE ALBULE—VILLA ADRIANA—TIVOLI
VILLA D'ESTE—VILLA GREGORIANA

Immediately upon leaving Rome (the bus starts in Via Gaeta), the cypresses of Campo Verano and the Basilica of S. Lorenzo (p. 103) appear on the right. The station, Bagni di Tivoli, is the entrance to *Acque Albule*, a much frequented sulphurous spa with swimming pools, which was known to the ancient Romans. From the Villa Adriana station a fine cypress-lined path leads to the *Villa of Hadrian*, the largest and most splendid of the villas of the Empire, the ruins of which are preserved. Its area is almost 175 acres. It was built by Hadrian during 125-135, making some use of previous constructions. Hadrian was an enthusiastic admirer of classical Greece and Egypt, and he wished to unite in his villa reminiscences of all the places to which he had grown attached in his travels. In

VILLA ADRIANA

272 A.D. part of the villa was assigned by Emperor Aurelian to Queen Zenobia of Palmyra as a place of exile. Many works of art excavated on the site of the villa have found their way to European museums.

From the entrance, an avenue of cypresses leads to a small Greek theater. Skirting the back of its stage, we ascend to the right through an avenue of cypresses to the *Poicile* (the name is a reminiscence of the Stoa Poicile, or Painted Hall, in Athens), a large garden surrounded by colonnades with a pool at its center. The wall at the north, over 220 yds. long and 28 ft. high, is exactly oriented from west to east. Along it ran colonnades, so that sunlight or shade could be had at pleasure. Next to the northeast corner of the Poicile, access through the Sala dei Filosofi, a chamber fitted with niches for statues, into the so-called *Teatro Marittimo*. This is a circular building, about 140 ft. in diameter, with an Ionic hall and a small island built at the center of a pool—probably a dining pavilion. The narrow wall of the Poicile on the northeast gives access to an olive grove, called the Stadium, at the west of which are first the smaller and then the larger Baths. Slightly to the west of these is a long and narrow valley called Canopus, an imitation of a canal near Alexandria in Egypt. At the end of the valley is a large niche with a fountain. Beyond, subterranean chambers, in imitation of the Temple of Serapis at Canopus near Alexandria. A large proportion of the sculpture in the Egyptian museum of the Vatican comes from these chambers.

From the northwest corner of the Teatro Marittimo, to which we now return, we gain access to the adjoining rooms of the Principal Palace. We enter first a slightly elevated rectangular court. The left side, preserved up to its upper story, is the so-called library. From the so-called triclinium on the northeast there is a fine view of the Vale of Tempe and the countryside of Tivoli.

Tivoli is the successor of Latin Tibur, which long maintained its independence of Rome, until it received Roman civic rights in 90 B.C. In the late Republic and the Empire it was a favorite summer residence of wealthy Romans.

Turning left at the entrance of the city to the Piazza S. Maria Maggiore, we find, at the right of the church, the entrance to the *Villa d'Este*, the most magnificent of the many Renaissance villas in Italy. It was built, beginning in 1549, by Cardinal Ippolito d'Este, son of Lucrezia Borgia; the Cardinal was also the creator of the gardens of the Quirinal Palace in Rome (p. 116). Plans for the villa were designed by the highly imaginative Pirro Ligorio. It has suffered from air bombardment in the second World War. Through unimportant secondary rooms we reach the highest terrace, looking out on lofty old cypresses and the high spray of the principal fountain. Steps lead down to the Viale delle Cento Fontane, with its numerous small sprays and the constantly repeated heraldic device of the ancient house of Este, whose last heir, Franz Ferdinand, Archduke of Austria and heir apparent of the Austrian throne, was assassinated in Sarajevo in 1914. At the left of the principal stairway is the so-called Rometta, a play-ful collection of the chief monuments of Rome in minia-ture. At the right, the cool Grotto of Diana with fine old plane trees. Farther along is the intricately playing Fon-tana dell'Organo; originally a water organ played music and imitated the sounds of birds. Below it, tranquil pools, and at the north wall a statue of Nature, repeating the ancient many-breasted statue of Artemis of Ephesus.

We traverse the main street of the town and reach the bridge over the Anio. Here there is a view of the terrace containing two Roman temples of travertine, dating to about 100 B.C. The one is circular, with Corinthian col-umns, and the other is rectangular, in the Ionic order, with a porch of four columns; it is not known to what deities these temples pertained. At the left, after the bridge, is the entrance to the *Villa Gregoriana*. Its narrow landscaped paths lead upwards to the right to a view of the "new waterfall." Here the Anio plunges 354 ft., through a cut in the cliff made in 1825-1836 to avert the danger of inundation. Below there is a view of the old cliff of the Anio cascades, with remains of the earlier falls, and also of the poetic grotto scenery.

It is advisable, upon returning to the main road, to fol-low it somewhat farther to the left. Passing an uncom-pleted triumphal arch, we arrive, in about twenty-five minutes, at the small church of S. Antonio, where a ter-race affords wonderful views of the new waterfalls oppo-site, of the valley of the Anio, and of the Campagna.

LIST OF POPES

Adrian VI, 1522-1523
Alexander VI, 1492-1503
Benedict XIII, 1724-1730
Benedict XIV, 1740-1758
Benedict XV, 1914-1922
Boniface VIII, 1294-1303
Clement V, 1305-1314
Clement VII, 1523-1534
Clement VIII, 1592-1605
Clement XIII, 1758-1769
Clement XIV, 1769-1774
Gregory I, the Great, saint, 590-604
Gregory IV, 827-844
Gregory VII, saint, 1073-1085
Gregory IX, 1227-1241
Gregory XI, 1370-1378
Gregory XIII, 1572-1585
Gregory XVI, 1831-1846
Gregory XV, 1621-1623
Honorius I, 625-638
Honorius III, 1216-1227
Honorius IV, 1285-1287
Innocent II, 1130-1143
Innocent VIII, 1484-1492
Innocent X, 1644-1655
Innocent XI, 1676-1689
John XII, 1316-1334
Julius II, 1503-1513
Leo I, the Great, saint, 440-461
Leo III, saint, 795-816

Leo IV, saint, 847-855
Leo X, 1513-1521
Leo XI, 1605
Leo XIII, 1878-1903
Martin V, 1417-1431
Nicholas IV, 1288-1292
Nicholas V, 1447-1455
Paschal I, saint, 817-824
Paul I, saint, 757-767
Paul II, 1464-1471
Paul III, 1534-1549
Paul IV, 1555-1559
Paul V, 1605-1621
Pelagius II, 579-590
Pius II, 1458-1464
Pius III, 1503
Pius V, 1566-1572
Pius VI, 1775-1799
Pius VII, 1800-1823
Pius VIII, 1829-1830
Pius IX, 1846-1878
Pius X, 1903-1914
Pius XI, 1922-1939
Pius XII, 1939
Sixtus III, 432-440
Sixtus IV, 1471-1484
Sixtus V, 1585-1590
Sylvester I, saint, 314-335
Symmachus, saint, 498-514
Urban VIII, 1623-1644

LIST OF ROMAN EMPERORS

Antoninus Pius, 138-161
Arcadius, 395-408
Augustus, 27 B.C.-14 A.D.
Aurelian, 270-275

Caligula, 37-41
Caracalla, 211-217
Claudius, 41-54
Commodus, 180-192
Constantine I, the Great, 306-337
Constantine II, 337-340

Diocletian, 284-305
Domitian, 81-96

Hadrian, 117-138
Honorius, 395-423

Julian the Apostate, 361-363
Justinian I, 527-565

Marcus Aurelius, 161-180
Maxentius, 306-312
Maximian, 286-305

Nero, 54-68
Nerva, 96-98

Phocas, 602-610
Pupienus, 238

Septimius Severus, 193-211

Theodoric the Great, 493-526
Theodosius the Great, 379-395
Titus, 79-81
Trajan, 98-117

Valentinian II, 375-392
Valentinian III, 425-455
Vespasian, 69-79

LIST OF ARTISTS

Abbreviations: A. = architect, P. = painter, S. = sculptor; Bol. = Bolognese, Dan. = Danish, Engl. = English, Ferr. = Ferrarese, Flem. = Flemish, Flor. = Florentine, Fr. = French, Ger. = German, Gr. = Greek, It. = Italian, Pol. = Polish, Rom. = Roman, Sp. = Spanish, Ven. = Venetian.

Agoracritus, Gr. S. (5th c. B.C.) 132

Alberti, Leon Battista, Flor. A. (1404-72) 126

Alcamenes, Gr. S. (fl. 440 B.C.) 132

Algardi, Alessandro, It. S. & A. (1602-54) 47, 76, 84, 147, 160

Ammanati, Bartolomeo, Flor. A. & S. (1511-92) 109, 153

Angelico da Fiesole, Fra Giovanni, Flor. P. (1387-1455) 50, 53, 76, 158

Antonello da Messina, It. P. (c. 1430-79) 159

Antoniazzo Romano, It. P. (fl. 1461-1508) 75

Apollodorus of Damascus, Gr. A. (fl. 2nd c. A.D.) 31

Apollonius, Gr. S. (fl. 2nd c. B.C.) 59, 141

Aristeas, Gr. S. (fl. 2nd c. A.D.) 144

Arpino, Cavaliere d', Rom. P. (1560-1640) 146

Baciccio, Giovanni Battista Gaulli, It. P. (1639-1709) 74

Barocci, Federigo, It. P. (1528-1612) 51

Bassano, Jacopo (da Ponte), Ven. P. (1510-92) 160

Bellini, Giovanni, Ven. P. (c. 1430-1516) 50, 159

Bernini, Giovanni Lorenzo, It. A. & S. (1598-1680) 9, 41f., 44, 46, 64, 74, 83, 98, 105, 111f., 114f., 117, 128, 147, 156ff., 160, 172

Borromini, Francesco, It. A & S. (1599-1667) 9, 64f., 73, 78, 112, 126, 169

Botticelli, Sandro, Flor. P. (1445-1510) 55, 62, 158

Bramante, Donato, It. P. & A. (1444-1514) 42, 45, 48f., 63, 79, 83

Bril, Paul, Flem. P. (1564-1626) 136

Bryaxis, Gr. S. (4th c. B.C.) 132

Cambio, Arnolfo di, It. A. & S. (1232-c. 1301) 82

Canina, Luigi, Rom. A. (1795-1856) 156

Canova, Antonio, It. S. (1757-1822) 9, 44, 46, 48, 117, 157

Caracci, Bol. family of P.s (17th c.) 9

179

INDEX

185